TEAM
COACHING
EDGE

THE ULTIMATE GUIDE
TO COACHING TEAMS
TO HIGH PERFORMANCE

ALISON GRIEVE AND JENNI MILLER

First published in Great Britain by Practical Inspiration Publishing, 2024

© Alison Grieve and Jenni Miller, 2024

The moral rights of the authors have been asserted

ISBN   978-1-78860-584-7   (hardback)
       978-1-78860-540-3   (paperback)
       978-1-78860-542-7   (epub)
       978-1-78860-541-0   (mobi)

Every effort has been made to trace copyright holders and to obtain their permission for the use of copyright material. The publisher apologizes for any errors or omissions and would be grateful if notified of any corrections that should be incorporated in future reprints or editions of this book.

Want to bulk-buy copies of this book for your team and colleagues? We can customize the content and co-brand *Team Coaching Edge* to suit your business's needs.

Please email info@practicalinspiration.com for more details.

Practical Inspiration Publishing

Contents

About the authors

Alison Grieve and Jenni Miller work with leaders and their teams in organizations of all sizes to help transform company culture and create differentiated performance. They train professional coaches and facilitators in the art and science of team coaching, sharing their extensive experience and knowledge. They are authors of the best-selling book *Leading Edge: Strategies for developing and sustaining high-performing teams* and present the regular podcast on leading high-performing teams: 'The Edge'. They regularly appear as keynote speakers and guests on podcasts and webinars. They won five awards in 2022–2023, including the Stevie Awards for Women in Business for Company of the Year.

Alison is a founding director at Management Dynamics and an experienced team coach, working with leaders and teams in some of the most successful businesses on the planet. She is an Advanced Certified Team Coach (ACTC) with the International Coaching Federation (ICF), a Korn Ferry master associate, an NLP Master Practitioner, a certified executive coach (ICF PCC) and a lead for the Team Coaching Faculty for Management Dynamics' Advanced Certification in Team Coaching programme.

Jenni is also founding director at Management Dynamics, a member of the Management Dynamics Team Coaching Faculty and a highly experienced and sought-after team coach. She has a huge depth of experience in the talent, leadership and organizational development areas. An Advanced Certified Team Coach (ACTC) with the International Coaching Federation, she has a postgraduate diploma in learning and development, is a certified NLP trainer and a certified coach (ICF ACC).

Together, through extensive research and direct experience with leaders and teams, Alison and Jenni have developed a methodology for collaborative intelligence. This transforms how leaders and teams operate, enabling sustainable high performance. They have a thriving team coaching practice and develop coaches through their ICF accredited Advanced Team Coaching with Advantycs® programme.

Introduction

Teams have stood the test of time and remain the lifeblood of any organization. However, their operational context has undergone significant changes in recent decades, and this transformation will only accelerate as the world becomes more complex, interconnected and ambiguous. In today's landscape, teams represent a massive competitive advantage – individual capability is no longer enough. While organizations invest in their people's development, motivation and rewards, tapping into the power of collaboration is the key to achieving something greater, more impactful and more powerful than what can be accomplished alone.

Many organizations excel at unleashing the potential of their individual employees. Yet, they recognize that to gain a competitive edge and execute strategies with the required innovation, complexity and speed, it is essential to unlock the potential of individuals working together harmoniously as a high-performing team.

Collaboration is on the rise, with people now dedicating 50% more time to working with others compared to two decades ago and spending 80% of their time on collaborative tasks. Hybrid working, which requires excellent collaboration, is now the most common work pattern for remote-capable employees.[1] Despite these trends, true collaboration remains elusive in most organizations, and its benefits are unevenly distributed. A mere 3% to 5% of employees contribute 20% to

---

[1] www.gallup.com/workplace/511994/future-office-arrived-hybrid. aspx?utm_source=workplace&utm_medium=email&utm_campaign= gallup_at_work_send_1_october_10102023&utm_term=newsletter& utm_content=heres_gallups_latest_analysis_and_advice_textlink_1

35% of value-added collaboration, drawing recognition for their capability and willingness to help and earning pivotal roles in projects.[2]

Organizations aspire to unlock the capacity of all team members, not just a select few, and tap into the power of widespread, inclusive teamwork. Research and experience demonstrate that high-performing teams can achieve significantly superior results compared to independent individuals.[3] By fostering a collaborative culture and harnessing the potential of collective effort, organizations can triumph in an increasingly dynamic and challenging business environment.

The growth of the team coaching industry

The coaching industry is growing fast – it was estimated to be $11bn globally in 2019, and is projected to almost double to nearly $21bn by 2030.[4] When surveyed on their thoughts about coaching, leaders demonstrated a satisfaction rate of 95%, which underlines how effective individual coaching can be. A total of 97% of organizations believed that implementing coaching had an impact on their employee's performance, while 80% of organizations globally use coaching in some way.[5] All of this demonstrates the growing desire for coaching and the credibility that coaches now have in the organizational context. Coaching is finally an accepted

---

[2] https://hbr.org/2016/01/collaborative-overload

[3] Abdullah Almaatouq, Mohammed Alsobay, Ming Yin, and Duncan J. Watts, 'Task complexity moderates group synergy', (2021).

[4] https://blog.gitnux.com/business-coaching-industry-statistics/#:
~:text=Conclusion-,The%20business%20coaching%20industry%20is
%20a%20rapidly%20growing%20sector%2C%20with,reach%20%2420.9
%20billion%20by%202030

[5] www.institutelm.com/resourceLibrary/creating-a-coaching-culture-2011.html

methodology for developing individual team members, and senior leaders increasingly want their whole team to be able to benefit from the coaching process, not just a select few individuals.

The team-building industry is also large, estimated to be approximately $3bn globally in 2022, and predicted to grow to almost $10bn by 2028.[6] The convergence of team building and coaching creates the team coaching approach, which responds to a pull from organizations to go beyond just an away day or fun team exercise. They want a focus on sustainable, increased performance and productivity which these experiences just cannot deliver.

The changing face of leadership development

In the past, organizations have emphasized the role of leaders as crucial to individual performance. They have established performance management, reward and recognition systems where leaders oversee their direct reports individually. Leadership development programmes have primarily concentrated on the leader's ability to impact one direct report at a time. Occasionally, there has been a focus on visionary skills, which involve influencing large groups of people. However, within this paradigm, the leader assumes complete responsibility for the performance of the entire group reporting to them.

We are witnessing a noticeable shift in this perspective, moving towards teams assuming mutual accountability for their own performance, leveraging interdependence and reducing siloes. This shift is characterized by a flatter hierarchy and enhanced collaboration. The role of the leader is

---

[6] www.linkedin.com/pulse/2030-team-building-service-market-size-2023-swot/

evolving into that of an enabler for their team – a person who creates an environment conducive to high performance and works with the team to maintain it.

Leaders possess a unique perspective of the team and their context, along with access to more resources than other team members. Despite this advantage, the leader is considered an integral part of the team, just like any other team member. In this new paradigm, the team collectively generate the desired outcomes, and the leader acts as a catalyst, facilitating the team in achieving their goals.

With all of this in mind, conventional leadership development methods are no longer fit for purpose. A fresh approach is necessary, and team coaching emerges as a powerful solution. Team coaching nurtures both the leader's pivotal role within the team and the team's overall performance improvement by focusing on the dynamics of the team.

The core emphasis lies in developing the mindsets of both the leader and the team simultaneously. Only after these mindsets have been transformed can one effectively cultivate the necessary skills in the leader and the team to sustain high performance. Team coaching addresses the holistic growth of the leader and the team, in the context of the system in which they operate, fostering a powerful and sustainable development process.

The changing team landscape

Teams are more complex than ever before because team members are more likely to be part of more than one team (e.g. in a matrix organization, task forces, project teams). This creates competing loyalties and priorities which challenge teams to be high performing. Gone are the days of simple reporting lines, one manager, clear and static job descriptions and longevity in role. Most people experience multiple reporting lines with several managers and fast-changing roles. This is a reality for teams, and they need to find a way to be high performing despite this context. It's not going to go away – if anything it will just get more complex and move even faster than ever before. Team coaching unlocks the potential of teams who work in this way by helping them find strategies to be high performing in a complex world.

What can high-performing teams achieve that individuals can't?

High-performing teams can achieve several things that individuals working alone cannot: they solve complex first-time problems; they anticipate and respond to change better; they make better decisions; they motivate each other; they are more innovative; and they create a sense of belonging and community.

They solve complex first-time problems

Increasingly, organizations are coming up against problems they've never seen before. High-performing teams are the secret to solving them again and again. The multiplier effect of several people working together, bouncing ideas off each other, sharing different perspectives, challenging ways of thinking and taking risks enables the team to come up with solutions that have never been tried before.

They anticipate and respond to change

The world is changing at an unprecedented pace with increasing amounts of ambiguity. Long gone are the days of predictable patterns of things like economic outlook, political stability, customer behaviour and technological progress, to name but a few. Individuals can achieve some success in analysing all these factors, drawing some conclusions and adapting to impending change. However, individuals will miss critical factors that teams of diverse thinkers and experiences will notice. Organizations are systems and only teams can create the impact required to change systems sustainably.

They make better decisions

Research tells us that teams make better decisions than individuals alone.[7] This is because teams will debate and brainstorm options more effectively than one person will on their own. It's also because many decisions require complex thinking which is impossible for people to do on their own – it requires different skillsets, perspectives and knowledge. High-performing teams ensure that they have great diversity of thought and skills, coupled with solid decision-making processes, which enable them to create superior outcomes.

They motivate each other

Individually, some people can be very self-motivated and driven. However, according to Gallup, only 21% of employees globally are engaged and low engagement alone costs the global economy $7.8 trillion.[8] High-performing teams are, in our experience, more engaged because they tend to motivate

---

[7] www.forbes.com/sites/eriklarson/2017/09/21/new-research-diversity-inclusion-better-decision-making-at-work/?sh=68bcdc674cbf

[8] www.gallup.com/workplace/349484/state-of-the-global-workplace.aspx?campaignid=18945816141&adgroupid=143633586437&adid=63 5680356863&gclid=CjwKCAjw1MajBhAcEiwAagW9McxXEXkRzNsp rNich4eeYiHk--AQ86TBG-cIzRG0wZAYEXMtMioa4hoCeWAQAvD_ BwE#ite-393245

each other and achieve better results together. Being part of a high-performing team creates the conditions for both intrinsic and extrinsic motivation, so much so that people are reluctant to leave high-performing teams. You'll also find that word gets around and people outside of the team want to join them.

They are more innovative

According to McKinsey, 84% of CEOs believe that innovation is critical to their organizational growth.[9] However, it's unlikely that individuals possess all the critical capabilities required to deliver innovation initiatives effectively. Innovation requires vision, curiosity and execution skills, all of which necessitate the collaboration only a high-performing team can achieve.

They have a sense of belonging and community

Organizations create some sense of belonging – for example, being part of something bigger than just yourself. Many have quite strong cultures which people enjoy and which create a feeling of community. However, the greatest source of belonging and community happens at the team level – the people you work with on a day-to-day basis. Some say that people join organizations and leave managers; we would extend this and say that people join organizations but leave managers and teams. High-performing teams recognize this and create strong bonds and a sense of community that only accelerate performance and well-being. While high-performing teams can be working in very stressful contexts, this community enables them to deal with their stress more effectively.

---

[9] www.mckinsey.com/capabilities/strategy-and-corporate-finance/how-we-help-clients/growth-and-innovation

High performance is by design

Any team can be a good team with a little bit of luck, a good leader and positive intentions from team members. However, it's impossible to be a high-performing team and sustain it indefinitely without putting effort into the team. A high-performing team is created by design and continuous focus on the conditions for success. This is where the power of team coaching really comes into its own – coaching challenges a team to accelerate their achievement of high performance and then sets them up for success in sustaining it. We explore this more in Chapter 2.

How to use this book

This book is designed to help you understand what team coaching is and the skills required. It also gives you a powerful methodology for effectively coaching teams, including a set of principles and conditions for success in teams, a coaching process, a diagnostic tool and a number of tools which you can access via our website.[10]

In writing this book, we have assumed that you are already an experienced individual coach and that you have some level of facilitation skill. Because of this, we don't cover these skills in much detail. We focus on what you need as a team coach and how you utilize coaching and facilitation skills in your team coaching practice.

The book is in two parts. In Part 1, we explore the essentials of team coaching which includes what team coaching is (Chapter 1), why it's useful (Chapter 2), the competencies of a team coach (Chapter 3) and how to develop your team coaching practice (Chapter 4).

---

[10] https://management-dynamics.com/teamcoachingedge

In Part 2, we look at EDGE Team Coaching using the Advantycs® framework. We start by introducing Advantycs®, then we introduce the Edge Dynamics of Reason, Results, Routines, Relationships and Resilience (Chapter 5). In this chapter we also discuss how to use diagnostics to coach a team to develop insights and track progress. In Chapter 6, we introduce the Seven Principles of EDGE Team Coaching – principles which you should constantly bear in mind when working with teams. In Chapter 7 we share the EDGE Team Coaching Process, which helps you to structure your team coaching engagements. We then look at creating a team Reason (Chapter 8), delivering team Results (Chapter 9), building team Routines (Chapter 10), deepening team Relationships (Chapter 11) and sustaining team Resilience (Chapter 12). Each chapter provides a good understanding of the relevant Edge Dynamic and how it supports a team's performance. It also includes some tools to help you coach a team on that Edge Dynamic, and insight about how the Edge Dynamics interact with each other.

Throughout the book you will find case studies, reference to tools and resources which you can use with your team coaching practice – these can be downloaded free of charge on our website: www.management-dynamics.com/team-coachingedge. Each chapter also has a summary at the end which you can use as a powerful reference tool. If you ever need a quick reminder of the topics in the chapter, use this! You don't need to read the book in consecutive order. It is written so that you can use it as a reference guide and dip in and out as you need to.

PART 1

Team coaching essentials

CHAPTER 1

What is team coaching?

In this chapter, we explore:

- What team coaching is and isn't
- How team coaching is similar and different to coaching individuals
- The role of the team coach

Defining team coaching

Team coaching is using coaching techniques to enable a team to achieve high performance and sustain it over time. The International Coaching Federation (ICF) definition is 'partnering in a co-creative and reflective process with a team and its dynamics and relationships in a way that inspires them to maximize their abilities and potential in order to reach their common purpose and shared goals'.[11]

In order to do this a team coach will use good coaching practice to identify the team's performance objectives and desired outcomes, establish where they are now in relation to those outcomes and then support the team to take action to fill that gap.

There's a lot of confusion amongst leaders, teams and coaches about what team coaching actually is. When we ask people what it is, they mention:

---

[11] https://coachingfederation.org/app/uploads/2021/10/Team-Coaching-Competencies_10.4.21.pdf

- Team building
- Training
- Consulting
- Mentoring
- Facilitation

All of these might be used as elements in your work with teams, but are not team coaching. Let's explore each of these in turn.

Team building

This historically has been the 'go to' for many teams when they want to develop. This might be away-days in the wilderness or team tasks which are designed to push the team to their limits. Social events might also come under this category. They can be great fun (or not, depending on how they are set up) but tend to be one-off and short-term focused. By the end of a day like this, you might have a highly bonded team who've had a great time together and shared a special experience. It's not team coaching, however, because there is no reflection and no action generated, and no follow up to maintain momentum from the insights generated. The ownership of the day sits with the person who is running the team-building session and not with the team.

Training

This is when a team needs to develop a particular skill or knowledge of something. For example, they might want to develop knowledge of a personality tool to use within the team. Or they might want to start working with a particular work process or learn how to improve their listening or communication skills. All of these things trigger training with a team, and they are not team coaching. This is because the trainer owns the process and is the expert on the content. They take the team through a curriculum of material and series of exercises and at the end of the training the team have developed their knowledge or skill in the area they are being trained in. Although the whole team might be attending the training together, it's not team coaching because it's trainer led. While you are trying to help the team to change their behaviour and do something different, you are doing so at the individual level by giving them some knowledge and helping them to practise a skill. This is very useful in a team context, but be clear, it's not team coaching. When you use that new-found knowledge and skill to evoke awareness across the whole team, you are back in team coaching territory.

Consulting

When you are working with a team you may stray into consulting. For example, you may help a team to devise their strategy, and when doing this the team could look to you for guidance and expertise. This is consulting, not team coaching. If you have the relevant expertise this could be useful to the team, but if not, be careful. Be clear what you are an expert in and what you are not. If you have expertise in business strategy in their industry, you have the credentials to step into consulting and to give them a wider perspective, share best practices from other organizations and industries and challenge some of their assumptions about their own business with all of this in mind. However, remember when you are doing this, you are not team coaching, you are consulting. The ownership of the content has shifted to you as consultant, and away from the team.

Mentoring

You may be working as a mentor with a team to share your experience or challenge the team to think a bit differently and support the team to grow. This is not team coaching because you are sharing your experience and knowledge rather than empowering the team to use their own resources and discover their own solutions. The ownership of the process sits with you as mentor, rather than with the team themselves. You are giving them the benefit of your knowledge. The process also tends to be more ad hoc rather than sustained over a period of time to support the growth of the team.

Facilitation

Without a doubt, you will be facilitating sessions of some sort in your work with teams. These may be in person or virtual and they are a core part of the work of a team coach. However, just facilitating a meeting for a team is not team coaching. In facilitation, you own the process in conjunction with the team which is usually agreed ahead of time and you facilitate a specific outcome for the team in that meeting, which might be agreement about a process or defining their strategy or many other things, but it is a one-off outcome which, once achieved, ends the process. Facilitation encourages dialogue with a team, usually with the outcome of creating clarity about something specific. You may facilitate more than one session with the team over time, but they are seen as separate incidences rather than part of a longer journey which is anchored back to the overall performance of the team.

So, if it's none of these things, then what is it?

Longer term

Team coaching is not a quick fix. There may be quick wins to be had but team coaching takes a longer-term view, usually a minimum of three months but up to 12 months is common. This is because you are working at the root-cause level of a team and their performance. You are also coaching a team of people to change how they work and behave. People are, by their very nature, complex and change at different paces, so it will naturally take some time. Team development is also about creating new habits in the team. Habits take time to break and establish.

As a team coach you are helping to raise self-awareness in the team. Teams will have varying levels of awareness of their own dynamics and what needs to change. Team members will have different perceptions of what high performance is, what the team is aspiring to achieve together and different levels of buy in to that aspiration. You may encounter initial resistance or cynicism within the team which needs to be overcome before any change will take place. All of this can take time and sustained effort. The leader and sponsors of the team need to understand that the time element of team coaching is an important consideration. A high-performing team is not created in one session. It's not a 'once and done' thing.

A partnership

Team coaching is a partnership between you as team coach and the team. The ownership of the process, and therefore accountability for the outcome they desire, sits with the team, not with you. You just coach them through the process and create the conditions for them to be accountable for their outcome. The partnership approach comes to life really effectively when you build an environment in which the team feel safe and explore the behaviours they would like to establish in their day-to-day work. Then they create actions which embed these behaviours and enable their growth as a team.

Team led

In team coaching, as we've mentioned, the ownership and accountability of the process and outcomes sits with the team. It's important here to think about what the team is. It's not a collection of individuals, all of whom you have individual relationships with. As team coach, your relationship is with the team as a single entity, leader included. You will have a special relationship with the leader, but you should be thinking about the team as a whole. The desired outcomes, the way in which they want to get there and their priorities for action all sit with the team as a whole.

Sustainable high performance

Team coaching is about creating long-term, sustainable performance which requires the team to take accountability for their continued development, without you present. Everything you do as team coach should have sustainability in mind. How do you enter and eventually exit from the team-coaching process and leave the team empowered and able to coach themselves? For example, over time a team should be able to run their own reflection sessions to review how they're doing as a team, the dynamics within the team and identify actions to shift their behaviour. Team coaching which doesn't do this is just creating dependence on you as a coach for their future performance.

Focuses on the dynamics in the team

Team coaching focuses in particular on the dynamics within the team. As a coach, you will always have one eye on the interactions between team members and whether they are effective, healthy and supporting the outcome that they are aspiring to achieve. Having a framework like Advantycs® (see Part 2) is invaluable as it articulates the conditions for success in a high-performing team. This helps you to coach the team on the things that will matter most to them. You can do this by raising the team's awareness of their own dynamics so that they can prioritize what to work on.

The links to individual coaching

There are many similarities between team coaching and coaching individuals. As a team coach you will draw upon all of the same skills and competencies that you would apply at an individual level. There are, however, several competencies you will need to add to your skillset in order to be a great team coach and we explore this in Chapter 3 of this book. You may recognize the following ICF Core Competencies[12] from your individual coaching practice:

- Demonstrates ethical practice
- Embodies a coaching mindset
- Establishes and maintains agreements
- Cultivates trust and safety
- Maintains presence
- Listens actively
- Evokes awareness
- Facilitates client growth

---

[12] https://coachingfederation.org/credentials-and-standards/core-competencies

The complexity of team coaching is that you are coaching several individuals as a single entity. As you know from your individual coaching practice, people are complicated beings and when you multiply that complexity by the number of people and interactions in the team, you get a very complex picture! This means that, as a team coach, you will also need to manage a group process, work with the team dynamics, run group exercises to evoke awareness and enable the team's growth as a whole. Creating an environment of trust and safety in a group is more challenging than in individual coaching but just as important to the outcome. You will not only need to think about the rapport you have with the team, but also how to enable the team to develop their rapport with each other.

Flexing between coaching and other modalities

In addition to your team coaching practice, you will undoubtedly use other modalities such as training and team building at times. These are useful methods for helping a team to develop skills and awareness and can be an excellent catalyst for evoking awareness in a team as long as you help the team to make connections and create insights from them, aligned with their contracted objectives. If you do bring these modalities into your team coaching, make sure you have the relevant skills. For example, if a team would like training on a personality tool, ensure you are certified in that tool before delivering the training. Also be clear that you are not team coaching during the training session. If you don't have the skills, bring in a trainer for that session who can run it for you. Even if you do have the skills, sometimes there is a benefit to bringing in someone else to run it for you so that you can maintain your coach stance and observe the team dynamics from a different perspective. It's also an opportunity to role model collaborative behaviours for the team.

Facilitation skills are essential for a great team coach. This is about leading a group process for improved team dialogue, so being able to understand things like group dynamics, how to get everyone to participate, how to give instructions, how to manage energy within a group, how to build agreement and action are all critical facilitation skills for your success as a coach. When you mix together facilitation and coaching you move beyond the group process to gaining insight and growth for the team. This is what differentiates using facilitation skills in your team coaching practice from pure facilitation, where there is no focus on the team dynamics.

Role of team coach

It's important to remember what your role is as a team coach. You can easily become entangled and invested in the team when spending so much time with them. This can cause issues. For example, it can be hard to remain objective and you can easily become a part of or at the very least enable unhelpful dynamics in their team. The minute a team says to you 'it feels like you are a part of our team', alarm bells should be ringing. This is an indicator you have become entangled and too close to the team. A helpful mantra is 'you are just the team coach'. You are not a part of the team; you are working in partnership with them. Maintain your stance with some distance to avoid entanglements.

It can also be easy to develop close relationships with individual team members, the most obvious being your relationship with the leader. Be careful of these connections, it's important that you have rapport, but having 'favourites' in the team will not serve you or the team well. The team will pick up on this and it will impact the sense of trust and safety in your work with them. Avoid gossip and side conversations with team members. If you're approached by an individual team member, encourage them to share their thoughts with the wider team rather than you.

Occasionally you may be asked to coach individual team members within a team you are coaching. We would suggest that this is not appropriate and that you should invite another coach to support those individuals. Otherwise, you are getting too close to individual team members and it is almost impossible to maintain the objectivity you require for both the individual and the team.

What is team coaching? A summary

Team coaching enables a team to achieve high performance and sustain it over time.

There's a lot of confusion amongst leaders, teams and coaches about what team coaching actually is. When we ask people what it is, they mention:

- Team building
- Training
- Consulting
- Mentoring
- Facilitation

All of which might be used as elements in your work with teams, but actually are not really team coaching. So, if it's none of these things, then what is it?

- Longer term
- Partnership
- Team led

- Sustainable high performance
- Focuses on the dynamics in the team

There are many similarities between team coaching and coaching individuals. As a team coach you will draw upon all of the same skills and competencies that you would apply at an individual level. There are, however, several competencies you will need to add to your skillset in order to be a great team coach. You will also need to manage a group process, work with the team dynamics, run group exercises to evoke awareness and enable the team's growth as a whole.

Throughout your team coaching practice, you will undoubtedly use other modalities such as training and team building at times. These are useful methods for helping a team to develop skills and awareness and can be an excellent catalyst for evoking awareness in a team as long as you help the team to make connections and create insights from them. If you do bring these modalities into your team coaching, make sure you have the relevant skills or bring in someone with those skills for the session.

When team coaching it's important to remember what your role is. Because you can spend so much time with a team, you can easily become entangled and invested in the team which can cause issues. Remember, you are just the team coach.

CHAPTER 2

High performance team coaching

In this chapter we explore:

- What high performance is
- What a high-performing team looks and feels like
- The three things a high-performing team brings to an organization
- The benefits of high performance to organizations, individual team members and leaders
- How high performance is by design
- Why you should become a team coach

What is high performance?

When we talk about high performance, teams often ask us what we mean – how do we define it? Many teams assume, at first, that performance is all about the numbers, the Key Performance Indicators (KPIs) or the objectives that the team needs to achieve. And that seems quite intuitive, doesn't it? Surely the organization measures a team's success in this way? Our challenge to those teams is to ask the question: 'And if your team is meeting your objectives, but it feels awful to be a part of this team, is that OK? Is that still high performing?' And the answer is always 'no'. In our view, high performance – coaching the team to fulfil their potential – must include not just achieving some objectives but also great Edge Dynamics (see Part 2 of this book for more details) in the team – *why* they exist, clarity on *what* they need to deliver and *how* they work together to get things done. When these two aspects – achievement of objectives and great Edge Dynamics – are present in a team, they can not only achieve or exceed their objectives, they can also sustain that level of achievement over a long period and through challenging times.

Most teams find it hard to articulate what high performance would look like for them. They also may worry that higher performance means more work. This is just not the case. In fact, higher performance should mean working smarter, not harder. Many teams are not far removed from this and could therefore be described as good teams. It won't take much to get them to high performance, but this doesn't happen by chance. When a team unlocks their potential, their motivation becomes self-sustaining.

Bringing high performance to life

So, what does it look and feel like when a team is high performing? We observe the following things in a high-performing team:

- The team delivers consistent, impressive results
- Team members are prepared to go the extra mile for the team
- There is a real cohesion and energy about the team members, who enjoy opportunities to collaborate interdependently
- Team members talk with pride about the team
- Team members demonstrate an inclusive respect for others in the team and can talk about their strengths and weaknesses
- Team members support each other through tough times

- The team challenge each other to continuously improve and raise the bar, giving each other feedback on what is and isn't working
- The team members are keenly aware of their stakeholders and manage them actively

The need for high-performing teams

High-performing teams deliver at least three things to the organization – greater innovation, complex problem-solving and superior decision-making.

Greater innovation

Innovation is rarely achieved successfully by one person alone and it requires a team to make an idea a reality. Teams take an idea, make it even better and create a plan together to turn it into something tangible, with organizational benefits. It's about experimenting, taking risks, learning from mistakes and failures and embracing a mindset of possibility. Alone, one person can demonstrate some of these traits but is unlikely to be able to sustain it over time or realize the value to the business. One person might have a great idea but taking that idea from concept to reality requires teamwork; they can rarely (if ever) do it alone. A high-performing team creates a playground for ideas – a space in which experimentation is embraced and risks are taken.

Complex problem-solving

One person can easily solve a simple problem by themselves. Complex problems, however, require different methods of approaching the problem. High-performing teams thrive on solving complex problems and utilize the strengths of the team to achieve a better solution. They use the diversity of perspectives in the team as well as the mental capacity of the whole team to approach a problem from a different angle.

Superior decision-making

High quality, timely decision-making is essential in organizations – if decisions are made too late or if they are not made well, organizations fail. Often, we see teams who struggle to make decisions, have repeated conversations and don't move forward. Or we see leaders who are bottlenecks for decisions because their team defer all decision-making to them. We also see teams who make decisions at the wrong level in the organization – leaders are focused on the tactical at the expense of the strategic and disempower the people they lead. High-performing teams consistently make great decisions and they do this through trust, collaboration and constructive challenge. They also make the right decisions quickly and efficiently. They ensure that decisions are high quality by considering diverse opinions. This is a fundamental building block of the competitive edge a high-performing team can deliver.

Organizational benefits

The possible benefits of high-performing teams are well researched and documented. Organizations see a drop in employee turnover when teams are cohesive and engaged.[13] Teams create a sense of belonging, collaboration and achievement and so high-performing teams are an organizational lever to reducing turnover.

---

[13] Ken Blanchard, *Leading at a higher level: How to be a high-performing leader* (2010).

Resources are usually limited in organizations and, when talking about this, we include money, time, people and materials. High-performing teams make better use of the resources that they have and are more productive than other teams.[14] This is because high-performing teams think more creatively about how to use what they already have more effectively.

When people are part of a high-performing team, they are much more likely to be engaged, which means that they are more motivated and productive, which in turn delivers better organizational results.[15]

When people are more engaged, they are happier at work, which reduces absence and sickness.

As we've already established, complexity is an increasing part of our working lives and how to solve complex problems is a common organizational challenge. According to Ernst & Young,[16] 'Almost 9 out of 10 companies… agree that the problems confronting them are now so complex that teams are essential to provide effective solutions.' High-performing teams tackle complex challenges head on.

Individual benefits

By extension, the organizational benefits lead to positive impacts on individual team members. High performance is something that is enjoyed by everyone – after all, who doesn't want to be a part of a high-performing team? When someone has a team around them, supporting them, they can achieve so much more than on their own. They are able to get to their

---

[14] Liz Wiseman, *Multipliers: How the best leaders make everyone smart* (2017).

[15] Marcus Buckingham and Ashley Goodall, *Nine lies about work* (2019).

[16] In their 2013 study *The power of many: How companies use teams to drive superior corporate performance* (May 2013).

own performance edge and beyond more easily. A leader of a high-performing team doesn't need to have all the answers and nor does an individual team member, they can find the answer together. This means that they can take more risks, be more confident and achieve more together. This is where a team is greater than the sum of its parts.

The benefits to the leader

If a leader doesn't create a high-performing team, the full accountability for the performance of their team lies with them. The team will look to them for the answers to everything. They will find they are repeating themselves regularly and fire-fight problems. They will get copied in on every email, they will not be able to have a holiday without being contacted. Their diary will be full of meetings, most of which will leave them feeling that it wasn't the best use of their time. When a leader has a high-performing team, the team will be empowered to make the right decisions without them being involved. They will know when to involve the leader and will keep them sufficiently informed of issues without needing their direct input all the time. They can maintain all of this while the leader is taking time to rest and recharge. They will have time to think and to focus on the strategic issues that add massive value to the organization and people's perception of their leadership capability. When they lead a high-performing team it's easy to attract talent to the team – people will know about the reputation of their team and want to be part of it. They will also keep people in the team for longer, as the benefits of being part of a high-performing team create a deep sense of loyalty to and ownership of the team.

High performance is by design

Any team can be a good team with a little bit of luck, a good leader and positive intentions from team members. However, it's impossible to be a high-performing team and sustain it indefinitely without putting effort into the team. A high-performing team is created by design and continuous focus on the conditions for success. This concept is well accepted in the sporting world. A high-performing sports team has continuous focus on the conditions for success in their context and has a plan, which they regularly review, to develop themselves as a team.

High performance is not achieved through a one-off event – a team-building day can be fun but rarely has lasting impact and needs follow up and follow through to create change in the team. High performance is achieved through regular moments of focus on the team and their Edge Dynamics. This is why it's so valuable for a team to work with a team coach. The coach can:

- Accelerate the development of the team by helping the team to explore what high performance is for them, where they are in relation to that, how to take action and gain quick wins to close the gap
- Bring to the team's attention blind spots and hidden dynamics which the team may not have been aware of
- Empower the team to step up to mutual accountability for the team's performance together with the leader
- Keep the momentum going as the team learns about high performance and make the necessary changes they need to develop

- Support the leader to think about their role and impact on the team's performance
- Develop the team to create a routine of self-reflection and experimentation in relation to their performance to enable the team to sustain performance over time once the coach has exited from the process

Why be a team coach?

You're probably already coaching individuals in some way and you already enjoy seeing the impact you can have on others and the transformation that you can support them to achieve. Team coaching multiplies this exponentially – at least by the number of people in the team, but it also extends out to the wider organization and the team's stakeholders. The ripple effects can be massive. For example, when you are coaching a leadership team, the impacts of them developing to high performance are felt by the entire organization. Whatever happens at the leadership level cascades down into the hierarchy of the organization.

A team coach supports a culture change in a team, which has enduring and extensive effects. We all know how hard organizational culture change can be – it's like trying to turn a tanker – slow and steady. Often organizations try to change their culture from the bottom up, which is the most ineffective method. Working at the team level is most effective. Even if you're only working with one team in an organization, because they are their own eco-system, you can effect massive change for that part of the organization.

All of this is hugely satisfying, especially if you enjoy making a difference or seeing results.

High performance team coaching– a summary

High performance must include the team not just achieving some objectives but also great Edge Dynamics in the team – why they exist, clarity on what they need to deliver and how they work together to get things done. When these two aspects – achievement of objectives and great Edge Dynamics – are present in a team, they can not only achieve or exceed their objectives, they can also sustain that level of achievement over a long period and through challenging times.

High-performing teams deliver at least three things to the organization – greater innovation, complex problem-solving and superior decision-making.

Organizational benefits include:

- Delivery of superior results
- Reduced staff turnover
- Increases in cohesion and engagement
- A greater sense of belonging, collaboration and achievement
- Teams making better use of the resources that they have and being more productive

Individual benefits include:

- Better support
- Achieving more personally
- Taking more risks
- Increased confidence

Benefits to the leader include:

- Improved decision-making at the right level
- Time to focus on the strategic
- Ability to take breaks, rest and recharge
- Attracting better talent

Any team can be a good team with a little bit of luck, a good leader and positive intentions from team members. However, it's impossible to be a high-performing team and sustain it indefinitely without putting effort into the team. A high-performing team is created by design and continuous focus on the conditions for success.

Team coaching can be hugely rewarding because it can multiply the impacts seen in individual coaching exponentially – at least by the number of people in the team, but it also extends out to the wider organization and the team's stakeholders. The ripple effects can be massive.

CHAPTER 3

Core competencies of a team coach

In this chapter, we explore:

- Each of the core competencies of a team coach

These competencies are based on the ICF Team Coaching Competencies, which are designed to integrate with and build on to the ICF Core Competencies. In this chapter we aim to bring each competency to life and give practical examples of how they show up in team coaching. We would highly recommend downloading the full team coaching competencies from the ICF website.[17]

Demonstrates ethical practice

This competency is all about your ethics as a team coach. This is about demonstrating personal integrity and honesty in your interactions with the team and their stakeholders. It's being considerate of the team's identity, culture and context. It's using respectful language consistently. It's following the ICF Code of Ethics[18] and upholding the Core Values.[19] It's

---

[17] https://coachingfederation.org/credentials-and-standards/team-coaching/competencies
[18] https://coachingfederation.org/ethics/code-of-ethics
[19] https://coachingfederation.org/app/uploads/2022/01/ICF-Core-Values.pdf

about maintaining confidentiality with all stakeholders as per the agreement you make with them.

It's also being clear about who the client is – the team as a single entity. You will need to distinguish between the different modalities discussed in Chapter 1 and only use them if you have the appropriate skill and expertise. It's about using those modalities only in service of the team's desired outcomes and being really transparent when doing so.

Coaches the client as a single entity

The team is made up of a collection of individual team members plus their leader. As a team coach, you need to consider the leader as a team member with a unique role and authority over the rest of the team. You will develop a relationship with the leader because you will work with them more closely than with any other team member. However, remember that this relationship and work that you do with the leader is in service of the team as a whole.

When meeting the team, be clear in your mind that you are working with them as a single entity. Be careful of developing close 1-2-1 relationships with team members apart from the leader. Team members may want to have a special relationship with you or to be coached by you individually. This is an entanglement which doesn't serve the team and should be avoided. If team members need 1-2-1 coaching, bring in another coach to do this. Often when you start working with a team, they might not see themselves as a single entity yet and just all work for the same leader without any other real connection. If you see them as a single entity, they are much more likely to become one. Help the team to notice this early on in your team coaching engagement and design your approach to help them become a team with a single unique purpose and sense of identity.

Maintains the distinction between team coaching and other modalities

Most team coaches have many areas of expertise such as training, facilitation, team building and mentoring. We discuss these and how they are different from team coaching in Chapter 1. None of these modalities are team coaching in their own right but it may be appropriate to bring them into your work with the team at various times to support their growth and achievement of their desired outcomes. However, it's important to maintain the distinction between these modalities and team coaching.

Demonstrates the knowledge and skills to practise the team development modality being offered

If you bring different modalities into your team coaching practice, you must have the relevant knowledge and expertise to do so. For example, if you use a personality assessment, you should have a certification in that tool, or bring in someone else who does to run that part of the session. Otherwise, there is a danger of delivering that session poorly and undermining the development of the team. The potential impact of a tool like this can be massive on a team but it needs to be done well to capitalize on it fully.

Adopts more directive team development modalities only when needed to help the team achieve their goals

In a team coaching process, because you are working with a group of people, there are times when a more directive approach is necessary to help the team achieve their goals or to increase awareness and learning. For example, you may run an exercise at the end of a team coaching session asking each team member to say one word about how they feel about the team right now. This is not team coaching, it is facilitation and is very directive. It's appropriate to use this exercise because it helps the team to raise their awareness of the feelings in the team and ensures that everyone is included in the process. You could bring the exercise back to team coaching by following it up with a question like 'what do you notice about the team as a result of this exercise?'

Maintains trust, transparency and clarity when fulfilling multiple roles relating to team coaching

When you use different modalities in your team coaching practice you should be clear with the team about what you are doing, why you are doing it and what your role is. Be clear how this relates to the team coaching process the team has engaged you for. For example, occasionally it may be important to develop the team's knowledge about a particular topic, such as trust and psychological safety in a high-performing team. Start by asking permission to share the knowledge by saying 'is it OK if I share a model?' If the team agrees, move into training modality and share the model you had in mind. Then transition back to team coaching by asking the team something like 'what comes up for you as I share that?' This ensures that you signpost clearly the transition between modalities for both yourself and the team.

Embodies a coaching mindset

This competency is all about your own mindset as a coach and the stance that you take in relation to the team and their accountability for their results. An effective team coach holds the position that the team is responsible for their own choices and the achievement of their desired outcome. A team coach continues to learn and develop and use reflective practices regularly. They are aware of the influence of context and culture on their team coaching practice. They use their self-awareness in a team coaching session to benefit the team. They manage their own emotions and state, preparing effectively to enable them to be present and have impact. They seek help from others when needed. They also have regular coaching supervision and remain objective and aware of team dynamics and patterns.

Engages in regular team coaching supervision

Because team coaching is demanding and complex, supervision is an even more essential part of your development as a team coach than in individual coaching. Supervision is reflective practice and a collaborative learning space with a professionally trained supervisor. They will challenge you to consider what impact your coaching practice is having and how you can maximize this. We would recommend supervision sessions every three months to maintain the level of reflection required to ensure your continued development.

Remains objective and aware of team dynamics and patterns

Remember, as we discussed in Chapter 1, you are just the team coach. As such, a core role you play is to remain objective and aware of the many dynamics in the team (e.g. power, control, expertise, misaligned goals, etc.) so that you can bring this to the team's attention, design an effective process and challenge the team's assumptions and beliefs effectively. If you are entangled in the team and have lost your objectivity, you will be likely to collude with the team and reinforce the status quo rather than enabling their growth. For example, a team may invite you to join them for dinner after a team coaching session. This can be very flattering and fun; however, you are in danger of inserting yourself into the team's social dynamic, which may undermine your ability to maintain objectivity.

Establishes and maintains agreements

This competency is all about the agreements that you create with the team, the leader and other relevant stakeholders – your 'contracting'. You should be explaining, early on in the process, what team coaching is and is not. You should be creating an agreement with the team and other stakeholders about what is and isn't appropriate in the relationship, what's in scope for the team coaching and the responsibilities of everyone involved.

You will need to create an agreement on things such as logistics, fees, scheduling, duration, termination, postponement, confidentiality and inclusion of other team stakeholders/experts.

One of the first things you will do is establish what the overall plan and goals of the team are. Take a partnership approach, with the leader and team being ultimately accountable for directing this.

Make sure that you are the right coach for the team. It is good practice to have a chemistry call with the leader prior to engaging with a team to ensure that you are compatible with the team and vice versa.

In every session you should be recontracting with the team on their focus points and what the outcomes should be within that particular session. All of this should be in service of their overall desired outcome as a team and should include measures of success. A successful team coach manages the time and focus of the team well and continues coaching in the direction of the team's desired outcome unless the team indicates otherwise.

A successful team coach also partners with the team to end the coaching relationship in a way that honours the experience (we discuss this in more detail in Chapter 7 when we discuss the 'Exit' stage of the EDGE Team Coaching Process).

Explains what team coaching is and is not

In the early stages of creating a partnership with your client team, it is important to explain to the leader, the team and other key stakeholders what team coaching is and is not and how it is different from other modalities. People have different expectations of team coaching: they may think that it is like a sports coach, who will tell the team what to do and how to improve. They may think that coaching is only for underperformance. They may think that as a coach you will share a lot of your experience and expertise. They may think that you will design an effective strategy for them. They may think that you will train them to be a better team. It's important to manage all of these possible misconceptions and to explain the power of team coaching and why this is ultimately the most effective way to accelerate their transformation to high performance.

Partners to collaboratively create clear agreements

A crucial part of the team coaching process is to create agreements (e.g. on confidentiality, how you will work and the scope of the team coaching process) with the team and all of their relevant stakeholders. When you don't do this well, you are in danger of misunderstandings, not managing expectations and ultimately not setting the team up for success to achieve their desired outcome. Consider how you help the team to incorporate the broader context in which they operate (e.g. the organizational culture, mission and climate) and their stakeholder's desired outcomes in the agreement that you create with them. For example, a team may say their desired outcome is to improve the dynamics within the team. But you've had conversations with the team's key stakeholder where they've told you the team needs to improve their results. It would be important to bring this to the team's attention and encourage them to incorporate the achievement of results into their desired outcome.

Partners with the team leader

When coaching a team, as we've discussed already, you will have a special relationship with the leader, and you need to establish the boundaries of that relationship and the role that you will play in team sessions in relation to the team and the leader. For example, it is not your role to give feedback to individual team members – that is the role of the leader or other team members. It's not your responsibility to resolve conflict in the team – that is the role of the leader or other team members. It's not your role to take on leadership of the team in any way – be careful of stepping into the leader's space and undermining them in or after team coaching sessions. For example, we would suggest it is good practice to let the leader have the first and last words in team coaching sessions. This re-establishes them as leader of the team and you an invited, objective guest. You are not part of their hierarchy. Consider how you signal the transfer of authority of the process in a team coaching session between yourself, the team and the leader. Contract all of this with the leader prior to the session and how they would like to show up for the team, which may be different than how they normally interact in the team on a day-to-day basis. Also contract with them how actions will be managed to ensure that they don't expect you to project manage them. This would only rob the team of accountability for them. Have in mind throughout the team coaching process that ultimately the team should be able to sustain high performance without a coach. Partner with the leader to achieve this.

Cultivates trust and safety

This competency is about two things – firstly, how you build and role model trust and safety between you as coach and the team. This is essential for a great coach–client relationship. Secondly, it's about how you create the conditions for building trust and safety between team members in team coaching sessions.

In order to build trust and safety the first thing you need to do is to understand the team's context. We discuss this in detail in Chapter 7 when we look at the EDGE Team Coaching Process. It's important to demonstrate respect for the team's identity, perceptions, style and language and to adapt your coaching accordingly. During the team coaching sessions, reinforce the team's unique talents, the insights they develop and the effort that they put into the coaching process. Show support, concern and empathy for the team while remaining objective. When team members share their feelings, concerns, beliefs and suggestions, acknowledge these as useful contributions. It's important to be open and transparent in your interactions with the team – role model the behaviours you are helping the team to develop such as vulnerability and trust.

Remember that trust develops over time and is in two stages – first reliability-based, then vulnerability-based trust. We discuss these more in Chapter 11. Think about how you demonstrate to the team in your first session with them that you are reliable, that they can depend on you and that you've got their back. Reliability-based trust is about establishing credibility – for example, sharing your credentials as a team coach with the team will help build your credibility with them and their belief that they are in safe hands. Once this has been established, you can move into developing vulnerability-based trust with the team by letting them know that imperfection is OK and that this is a learning process, so therefore a little bit messy. Ask for help if you need it, admit mistakes when you make them and role model vulnerability-based trust with the team.

Creates and maintains a safe space for open and honest interaction

There are many tactics for creating and maintaining a safe space within team coaching sessions, where team members feel safe to disagree and raise sensitive topics. For example, think about both the introverts and extraverts in the team and how to engage both personality types. Introverts think to speak whereas extraverts speak to think. Extraverts can therefore find it easy to contribute to team sessions but there is a danger that they can take up all of the team's airtime. Introverts often need time to reflect before contributing and may need to be specifically invited to share their opinion. Design your team coaching exercises with this in mind. Building in breakouts of smaller groups or pairs gives everyone the opportunity to contribute. Creating a reflective moment at the start of an activity or sharing questions before the session enables an introvert to formulate their thoughts before contributing in the session.

Another tactic is to agree expectations at the beginning of every team coaching session. Get the team to define these themselves and write them up and keep them visible throughout the session. For example, teams often mention behaviours like 'be respectful', 'listen to each other' and 'have a positive intent'. Remind the team of these expectations regularly. Check in on them throughout the session and ask them how they are doing against those expectations. This maximizes the chances of them being demonstrated. If you notice the team breaking the expected behaviours, bring it to the team's attention by saying something like 'remember you agreed an expectation of "be present", I've noticed a few people in the team appear to be distracted by their email, what would you as a team like to do about that?' This holds the team accountable for their behaviour.

One approach can be to brainstorm using sticky notes – this ensures that people can contribute equally and in the same way. The anonymity of writing it down and not having to say it out loud can create the safety needed to contribute when they might not otherwise have done so.

Promotes the team viewing itself as a single entity

We've already discussed in this chapter about how you need to view the team as a single entity and how they might not see themselves in this way at first. Teams often start as a bunch of individuals who all report to the same boss. They don't identify yet as a team beyond that hierarchical connection. In order to change their identity to a team as a single entity they need to identify why they exist as a team in the first place and what connects them all individually with each other. Use the Team Reason Creation Process (see Chapter 8) to help the team to establish their team Reason. Then, use the 'Big Whats' Process (see Chapter 9) to help them to identify their team Results and what they work together on interdependently. Both of these exercises promote the team viewing itself as a single entity with a common identity. Consistently promote the team's self-sufficiency so that they can sustain high performance over time without you coaching them.

Fosters individual team members' and the collective team's feelings and beliefs

Team coaching encourages everyone to speak freely and it's important for the coach to understand and clarify the collective feelings and perceptions of the team. In order to build vulnerability-based trust, team members need to share more about themselves than they would normally do. This is about them sharing how they feel, what they believe, what's important to them, what they aspire and hope for and suggestions for improvement. Many team coaching exercises in the Advantycs® toolkit enable this. For example the values exercise (see Chapter 8) helps team members to articulate what is most important to them at work and what might cause them to be demotivated, or at worst leave the team. Another exercise is Personal Success Stories[20] which helps team members to learn more about each other and give each other appreciative feedback and recognition. You could do a team check in with everyone at the beginning of a coaching session where you get team members to share how they are feeling in that moment.

Encourages participation and contribution by all team members

Effective team coaching involves enabling everyone in the team to share their opinions, knowledge and skills so that the team gets the full benefit. Have one eye on inclusion all the time. How inclusive a team is has been shown to be a core predictor of team success.[21] This is about equal contribution to team tasks and conversations. So, help the team to participate

---

[20] Download this tool from our website: www.management-dynamics. com/teamcoachingedge

[21] www.linkedin.com/pulse/hard-data-what-greatest-predictor-team-ef-fectiveness-tracey-lovejoy/

equally and contribute in team coaching sessions so that they take those behaviours into their daily work. Encourage them to invite each other into the conversation and value the contributions made. Every team exercise in the Advantycs® toolkit is designed in this way. Running a diagnostic regularly throughout the team coaching process ensures contribution by each team member in some way.

Partners with the team to develop, maintain and reflect on team rules and norms

Help a team to establish what their rules and norms are as a team. This should include things like how and when do they meet; how do they communicate; how should they behave with each other; how do they make decisions; how do they support each other and manage workload, etc.? Once established, help the team to take action to maintain these rules and norms and help them to create a routine to regularly check in on them. If they're not working, the team should change them. Bring to the team's attention, with permission, your observations about how they follow these rules and norms or not and then ask them what gets in the way. Coach them to reflect on what triggers them to stop following their rules. Challenge them to think as a team on how they could approach things differently in the future and support each other when triggers appear.

Promotes effective communication within the team

A key factor in any team's success is their ability to communicate effectively with each other. Being clear about what team members communicate with each other, how and when is essential. If the team has clarity of their team Results (e.g. they've completed the 'Big Whats' exercise[22] referenced in Chapter 9), they can establish what communication Routines (see Chapter 10) they employ to monitor progress and deliver those Results. To start with, the team might be tempted to communicate either with you as coach or to the leader rather than with each other. Gently encourage them to communicate with each other when you notice them doing this.

Partners with the team to identify and resolve internal conflict

High-performing teams are able to work with conflict when it occurs with the team. They know that an absence of conflict is as unhealthy for a team as destructive conflict, where there are no boundaries to their behaviour towards each other. The team can manage (but not avoid) these situations when they occur. We discuss all of this in detail in Chapter 11. Manage your own response to conflict when it occurs in the team. Notice whether you tend to avoid, get involved or mediate when conflict occurs as none are appropriate in a team coaching context. When conflict does occur, encourage the team to bring it to the surface constructively and then reflect on what there is to learn.

Maintains presence

This competency is all about how you manage your own state and therefore that of the team you are coaching. It's how you stay present, focused and observant throughout the team coaching process. It's about the space you take up physically

---

[22] Download this tool from our website: www.management-dynamics. com/teamcoachingedge

and mentally. It's how you demonstrate curiosity about the team's context, dynamics and assumptions. It's how you manage your own emotional reactions in the team coaching and how you demonstrate confidence in a wide variety of situations. It's about how you react when there is ambiguity in the team coaching process and it's being comfortable creating space for pause, silence and reflection. Start with yourself first and notice what's going on for you and it will be much easier to manage the state of the team.

First of all, why should we care about maintaining presence? Let's look at it through the lens of what happens if we don't successfully manage it. Most importantly, emotions can take over either you or the team. Emotions are useful feedback and should be noticed, but the minute they take over, you lose control of yourself and the room. Something might trigger you or a team member and it's important to be able to manage it.

Conflict can also happen in team sessions, either between you and a team member or between team members. Being able to maintain your presence is crucial to enable the conflict to be resolved and for everyone to move forward with new insights. State management is essential for this. If a team's state is not managed, they might start to feel bored, tired, there could be a sense of inertia, frustration or confusion. These can all get in the way of creativity and action.

Manage the team's state and they will remain focused, positive, creative and action oriented. There are three types of energies it's important to pay attention to: physical, so what's going on in yours and others' bodies; emotional, so what is going on for people emotionally; and mental, which is what people are thinking and saying to themselves (self-talk) and others.

Team coaching requires a lot of energy. In individual coaching, you're usually coaching people for shorter periods of time – often one to two hours at a time. And I'm sure you know how much energy it can take to maintain your attention and focus on one person for that length of time! Now, multiply that by the number of people you have in the team plus a longer duration of typically two to eight hours and you're going to have to maintain your presence for a long time! Manage your energy well to ensure you are always at your best in the coaching process. Using a co-coach can help you to manage your energy well as you can swap roles throughout the coaching process. It's also a fantastic opportunity to learn from each other.

In terms of mental energy, perhaps the most important part here is noticing and managing your own self-talk. What you are saying to yourself is a massive factor of your state. Just think about what impact it has when you say something negative to yourself like 'that was bad wasn't it?' – does it make you feel good and confident? Or does it have the opposite effect? When you notice you're saying things like this to yourself, stop and say something more constructive instead, like 'okay that wasn't the outcome I wanted, let's think about what I do next to create a better outcome'.

A useful tool for noticing your mental energy is when you step into an observer role in the room while you are delivering a session and notice how you are interacting with the participants and what impact you are having. Notice what's going on inside yourself as well as outside. This can help you to notice what's going on in the whole room as well as for yourself and the impact everything is having.

In terms of emotional energy, start by noticing and paying attention to your gut feelings. They are useful sources of information. They're not always right, but it's important to notice them and to decide whether to bring them to the attention of the team or leader or both and how to do so.

In terms of managing the state of the team, build state management into the session plan – plan a break every 90 minutes, or break sooner if the team looks like they need it. Regular breaks are incredibly important in team sessions. The participants will need breaks to manage all three energies. Without breaks, they get distracted by thirst, hunger or needing the bathroom. They will be more likely to get into emotionally charged conflict and they will struggle to think creatively and move forward.

Having the courage to hold up the mirror to the team about something that they weren't aware of until you helped them notice it is a key skill to develop. When else would they have the opportunity to notice this? Who else would give them this feedback? Probably never and no one. It's also having the courage to challenge the team about their assumptions and beliefs and bring them to their attention. These moments will pave the way for a shift in a team.

Constantly think about how you are partnering with the team, how you are coaching using the Seven Principles of EDGE Team Coaching (see Chapter 6). Be aware of what you are saying and doing and the impact it is having on the team at all times. Be very intentional about the questions you ask and the words you use as, in your team coach role, you have a huge impact on the team at all times. Your body language speaks volumes about your intentions and what you are thinking. The team are paying attention – all the time!

Uses the full range of sensory and perceptual abilities

We have a number of senses for a reason so use them all in your team coaching practice. Notice what you are seeing and hearing, but also notice what is not being said or done by the team. This is information too. Using techniques which broaden your perception of what is happening in the team can be really useful for managing the complexity of what is going on in the group dynamics.

Notice your own emotions as sometimes they can be a reflection of an emotion which the team is experiencing but not voicing. Check whether it's your own emotion – are you being triggered by something the team is talking about? Is it your own reaction or something you are reflecting back from the team? If it's the latter, how can you bring this to the attention of the team? Saying things like 'I'm noticing is a feeling of anxiety right now, what comes up for you as I say that?' ensures that you are just presenting it as your own feeling for the team to try on and notice whether they resonate with it or not.

Uses a co-coach when necessary

Sometimes it might be helpful to use a co-coach as this enables you to manage your energy more effectively and to notice and act upon the energy levels of the team. Having a co-coach also enables you to practise different skills in a team session and get feedback from your co-coach. We'd definitely recommend having a co-coach in teams of 15 or more people.

Encourages team members to pause and reflect

Teams are often highly action oriented, and the typical organizational context very often drives this behaviour. However, a team that jumps straight to action without reflection first will likely make poor decisions or not be fully committed to the actions they agree to. Encourage the team to slow it down a bit and to have times when they pause and reflect on what's happening in the team. For example, helping them to reflect on how the Edge Dynamics (see Chapters 8–12) are showing up in the team via a diagnostic and subsequent conversation can be extremely insightful and lead to transformation.

Moves in and out of the team dialogue

As coach it's important to know when to be a part of the team dialogue and when to step back and let the dialogue flow with minimal intervention from you. Ultimately, you are aiming for the team to be self-sufficient in their own coaching. So, the more they are capable of continuing a dialogue without your intervention, the better. However, to start with, most teams require a lot of powerful coaching questions from you to keep them on track with discussions about the team's performance. Otherwise, they may go down what we call 'rabbit holes' which are discussions that don't support the team's desired outcomes. Usually they are detailed, work-related or irrelevant conversations. When this happens, notice how many people are involved in the conversation and their body language. If some are disengaged from the conversation, it's a good idea to bring it to the team's attention that some are being excluded from the conversation so it may not be appropriate to discuss it now. When this happens, ask the team if the conversation is relevant to their desired outcome.

Listens actively

This competency is about listening to understand the team's context, identity and experiences. It's about summarizing to ensure clarity and understanding. You will probe to seek out whether there is more underlying what the team are communicating. It's about noticing emotions, energy, body language and other behaviours in the team. It's about identifying the full meaning of what is being communicated through the team's words, tone of voice and body language.

And it's about noticing trends and patterns in behaviour across sessions to discern themes.

Notices how the perspective shared by each team member relates to the team as a whole

It's important as a team coach to consider how individual perspectives are similar or different to others in the team and bring this to the attention of the team. Help the team to notice any emerging themes and whether or not they are shared across all the team. Also notice the reactions that other team members have to those perspectives and if appropriate bring this to the attention of the team. Some team members may have a different insight to the team dynamics than their colleagues – this is an opportunity to build on their insight and encourage the team to consider that point of view.

Notices how each team member impacts the collective energy, engagement and focus

Every team has team members who either generate energy, engagement and focus or sap it. Notice the impact each person has and what triggers an increase or decline in energy, engagement and focus. Is it because that person thinks very differently to the rest of the team? If so, how can the team appreciate and utilize that difference a bit more? Help team members to notice the impact of these behaviours and to change their response if needed.

Notices verbal and non-verbal communication patterns in the team

A team coach must pay attention to all communication from the team – no matter how subtle – both verbal and non-verbal.

What are these signals telling you about the dynamics within the team and how can you bring this to the attention of the team in a constructive way? Use all of your senses to notice the patterns during sessions and also calibrate what shifts from one session to another.

Models confident, effective communication and collaboration when working with a co-coach or other expert

When you invite other people to work with the team alongside you, you will need to demonstrate confident, effective communication and collaboration. This is a wonderful opportunity for the team to witness these behaviours in action and how impactful they can be. Every interaction with the team you are coaching can also be an opportunity to role model the behaviours the team are wanting to develop.

Encourages the team to own the dialogue

We talked earlier about you moving in and out of the dialogue and it's also important to encourage the team to own their dialogue. In order for a team to achieve sustainable high performance, they need to feel in charge of their own team coaching process. Right from the start of your engagement think about how you can encourage this. For example, give them control of the agenda and recontract with the team if things change. When the team is in a conversation, check in regularly and ask them if the activity is supporting them to achieve their desired outcomes. Help the team to establish processes for making effective decisions together (see Chapter 10).

Evokes awareness

This competency is all about the tools and techniques you use as a team coach to 'hold up the mirror' and evoke awareness in the team.

This competency is also about being able to challenge the team to gain insight or awareness of their thinking, their values, needs, wants and beliefs. It's about probing deeper, sharing more about and going beyond their current experience. It's also about noticing what helps the team progress and adjusting your coaching process to respond to their needs as a team. You will need to help the team to notice their current and future patterns of behaviours and thinking and invite them to come up with ideas about moving forward. A useful skill is reframing, which is about offering a new meaning to a statement or idea the team have come up with. It's also about sharing observations, insights and feelings without attachment to create new learning for the team.

Challenge the team's assumptions, behaviours and meaning-making processes

There are many techniques for challenging a team on their assumptions, behaviours and meaning-making processes. For example, reporting behaviour is a great tool. This is how you can bring to the attention of the team unhelpful behaviours. You could say something like 'I'm noticing we have only heard from three people so far…' or 'I notice some of you are multitasking, what can we do about that?' – the last bit of 'what can we do about that?' pushes the solution to the team.

Another tool is perception check. This is where you have noticed something, and you want to bring it to the attention of a team member or the team as a whole. Here you could say something like 'You appear to be upset' – this is said without judgement or certainty – you're not saying they are upset, just suggesting that they appear to be upset. You're not reading their mind. This gives them the chance to disagree with you and for it to be OK.

Assumption checking is another tool you could use. For example, a team might say to you 'what if it doesn't work?' – this has an underlying assumption associated with it that may or may not be true. Believing it will not work may not be helpful for the team, so you can challenge them by asking 'what makes you think that it won't work?' or 'what if it does work?'

Uses questions and other techniques to foster team development

The most powerful tool you have at your disposal as a team coach is questioning. Use open questions early on in your team coaching sessions to generate insights and evoke awareness in the team. The most powerful open questions usually start with a 'what' or a 'how'. Use more closed questions towards the end of your team coaching sessions when you want to generate action and commitment to that action.

Facilitates client growth

This competency is all about how you support the team to move forward through integrating new awareness and taking action. Help the team to integrate their learnings into their new way of working together. Support them to design effective actions and measures of success. It's about supporting the team to be autonomous and accountable for the achievement of their goals and actions. It's about supporting them to learn from their progress and results. Encourage them to move forward and identify roadblocks and potential barriers to their success. Work with the team to summarize what they have learned in between sessions. Celebrate their progress and success and partner with them to end each session well.

Encourages team dialogue and reflection

Every exercise you do as a team coach should either encourage team dialogue (discussion amongst the whole team about what is working well in the team, what could be different and how to do that) or reflection (thinking about what they've learned to gain insights into the team dynamics). Often well-designed exercises will enable both. The Advantycs® toolkit[23] provides over 30 tools to help you to coach a team with both dialogue and reflection.

Core competencies of a team coach – a summary

The ICF Team Coaching Competencies outline eight competency areas for team coaching practice:

Demonstrates ethical practice – this is all about your ethics as a team coach. This is about demonstrating personal integrity and honesty in your interactions with the team and their stakeholders.

Embodies a coaching mindset – this is all about your own mindset as a coach and the stance that you take in relation to the team and their accountability for their results.

---

[23] Find out more about the Advantycs® toolkit at www.management-dynamics.com

Establishes and maintains agreements – this is all about the agreements that you create with the team, the leader and other relevant stakeholders.

Cultivates trust and safety – this is about two things – firstly, how you build trust and safety between you as coach and the team. This is essential for a great coach–client relationship. Secondly, it's about how you create the conditions for building trust and safety between team members.

Maintains presence – is all about how you manage your own state and therefore that of the team you are coaching.

Listens actively – is about listening to understand the team's context, identity and experiences.

Evokes awareness – is all about the tools and techniques you use as a team coach to 'hold up the mirror' and evoke awareness in the team.

Facilitates client growth – this competency is about how you support the team to move forward through integrating new awareness and taking action.

Chapter 4

Developing your team coaching practice

In this chapter, we explore:

- Education and training to develop as a team coach
- Certification
- Continued coach education
- Being part of a team coaching community
- Developing your team coach toolkit
- Supervision
- Broadening your understanding of business models, systems and practices
- Turning up the heat and variety to develop as a coach

Education and training

Team coaching is an advanced skill and builds on the existing foundational skills of coaching and facilitation. Without these two skills, you will find team coaching almost impossible. If you have both skills already and plenty of experience under your belt both of coaching individuals and facilitating group sessions, then we would recommend the first step in your team coaching development is to attend an accredited training programme specifically aimed at developing team coaching skills. We would suggest looking for a programme which is accredited as an Advanced Accreditation in Team Coaching (AATC) programme, aligned with the ICF Team Coaching Competencies.[24] Also ensure that your programme consists of plenty of practise and feedback as this will develop your team coaching skills far more than the theory. Coaching is not an academic exercise so avoid any programme that treats it as such.

Certification

The team coaching industry is still very much in its infancy and so professional certifications, or credentials, for team coach practitioners are quite new. We would suggest it is highly worthwhile pursuing a team coaching certification with an organization like the ICF to demonstrate that you have a sufficient level of team coach education, experience and ongoing professional development to be working at this level. The ICF offers the Advanced Certification in Team Coaching.[25] This certification programme is well respected and increasingly organizations recognize its worth.

Continued coach education

Once you are certified as a team coach, in order to maintain your certification, you will need to complete a certain number of hours of continued coach education per year. Regardless of your accreditation status, we would assert that, as a development professional, you should be modelling good development practice yourself and continuing to learn every year. This involves increasing your knowledge, practising new skills, gaining new tools for your team coach

---

[24] https://coachingfederation.org/credentials-and-standards/team-coaching/competencies

[25] https://coachingfederation.org/credentials-and-standards/team-coaching

toolkit and keeping abreast of trends that are relevant to the coaching industry.

Being part of a team coaching community

Team coaching is often a solitary pursuit and so it can be hugely valuable to build and take part in a community of team coaches. A community is at its best when it encourages the sharing of ideas about team coaching and challenges members' thinking. Of course, a community could also be a source of potential co-coaches when needed. There are not currently many formal team coaching communities but alumni groups from team coaching programmes can work really well. You may need to invest time and effort in keeping the community alive and adding value, but it will be worth it. ICF offers the Team and Group Coaching Community of Practice that can support a team coach in developing a network of peers around the world.[26]

Developing your team coach toolkit

We've discussed a number of the Advantycs® tools in this book and you may already have other tools you use with teams in your back pocket. It is useful to keep on adding to your toolkit all the time. Be on the lookout for new tools – you can find them in all sorts of places such as articles and blogs. Working with a co-coach can introduce you to new tools or a different way of facilitating an existing tool. This variety will keep things fresh in your team coaching practice.

---

[26] More information is available at https://coachingfederation.org/communities-of-practice

You will need a whole range of tools for different purposes and different types of teams; don't be afraid to adapt a tool to suit the needs of the team you're working with and their context. One tool can work perfectly for one team but not the next. Think about their dynamics, their working style, their personality preferences and their team/organizational culture when designing your approach. This can be hard to ascertain the first time you work with a team, so pay attention to the leader, team members and what you notice about the dynamic of the team.

Every tool that you add to your toolkit should shift a team towards their desired outcome. Make sure that all the tools you use remain in the team coaching space most of the time. Select your follow-up questions carefully to bring an exercise back to team coaching and draw insights from the experience the team just had.

Personality tools can be a useful addition to your team coaching toolkit. Make sure that if you use them, you are accredited to do so as a rudimentary knowledge of a tool means a surface level approach to the insights a team can get from it. We use many personality tools in our team coaching practice and there are pros and cons for each of them which we won't go into here. What's important is using the insights a personality tool can give team members to help the whole team to consider what impact personality is having on the Relationships (see Chapter 11) in the team, and how they could adjust their Routines (see Chapter 10) to be even more effective based on personality traits. In fact, reviewing all the Edge Dynamics (see Chapter 5) through the lens of a tool like this can lead to significant transformation. In other words, if you're going to use personality tools, use them well.

Supervision

Supervision[27] is reflective practice with a professionally trained supervisor who will challenge you to consider what impact your coaching practice is having and how you can maximize this. Supervision is an excellent way to stretch your development as a team coach by growing your perspectives, awareness, objectivity, insight, approach and confidence. It should be an ongoing part of your coaching practice and you could take part in a group or 1-2-1. Supervision can be great at helping to look at yourself as a coach from a different perspective such as the 'fly on the wall'. Seeing yourself from an observer perspective can be insightful and a practice that you can use all the time, even when you are not being actively supervised. We would suggest this is a great technique to eventually use while you are in team coaching sessions to notice the impact you are having and how you could maximize this by being your own internal supervisor.

Broadening your understanding of business models, systems and practices

When working with teams, in order to establish your own credibility and to support them in the best way, you should have a broad understanding of the industry and business model your client teams operate in. Taking a systemic view is important, which means thinking about all of the interdependencies and influences the team has to consider. Where are the power, the handoffs, the reliances for this team? Who ultimately decides whether they exist or not? Be

---

[27] https://coachingfederation.org/credentials-and-standards/coaching-supervision

curious about all of this when you're working with a team as not only does it increase your ability to support them effectively, it also helps them to gain insights about the system they are working in and therefore how to influence and be more successful within it.

You will also need to have some awareness of core business practices and models such as Agile, Lean, Six Sigma, especially if your client team uses them in their work. Understand typical business cycles such as performance management or financial processes. Know what the biggest pressures are in certain industries such as time of year (e.g. in retail the run up to Christmas is usually insanely busy). Understanding all of this is about being able to demonstrate empathy with the team for the context they are operating in.

Limit your curiosity to mostly outside of your team coaching sessions. Spending a long time in a team coaching session with a team getting them to help you understand their context could be perceived as a waste of the team's time, especially when it's hard to get them together as a group. Embrace your curiosity outside of team coaching sessions. If you hear the team talking about a term you don't understand, ask for a quick clarification and make a note to look it up later.

Turn up the heat and variety

Working with the same types of teams all the time may be great for your confidence but in the end could be a detriment to your team coaching practice. To develop as a team coach, you will need to continuously stretch, which requires heat and variety. Heat is when you are a bit out of your comfort zone – there is a possibility of failure and that failure would be visible. For example, try things with teams that you've never done before and act as if you've done it many times.

Variety is about working with different types of teams – teams at different seniority levels, size of business, size of team, functions, industry, etc. Turning up both the heat and variety and coupling this with effective supervision and a great team coaching community will ensure that you continue to develop as an amazing team coach.

Developing your team coaching practice – a summary

Team coaching is an advanced skill and builds on the existing foundational skills of coaching and facilitation. Without these two skills, you will find team coaching almost impossible. If you have both of these skills already and plenty of experience under your belt both of coaching individuals and facilitating group sessions, then we would recommend the first step in your team coaching development is to attend an accredited training programme specifically aimed at developing team coaching skills.

We would suggest it is highly worthwhile pursuing a team coaching certification with an organization like the ICF to demonstrate that you have a sufficient level of team coach education, experience and ongoing professional development to be working at this level.

Regardless of your certification status, we would assert that, as a development professional, you should be modelling good development practice yourself and continuing to learn every year.

Team coaching is often a solitary pursuit and so it can be hugely valuable to build and take part in a community of team coaches.

It is useful to keep on adding to your toolkit all the time. Be on the lookout for new tools – you can find them in all sorts of places such as articles and blogs. Working with a co-coach can introduce you to new tools or a different way of facilitating an existing tool. This variety will keep things fresh in your team coaching practice.

An excellent coaching method, supervision is reflective practice with a professionally trained supervisor who will challenge you to consider what impact your coaching practice is having and how you can maximize this.

When working with teams, in order to establish your own credibility and to support them in the best way, you should have a broad understanding of the industry and business model your client teams operate in. Taking a systemic view is important, which means thinking about all of the interdependencies and influences the team has to consider.

To develop as a team coach, you will need to continuously stretch, which requires heat and variety. Heat is when you are a bit out of your comfort. Variety is about working with different types of teams – teams at different seniority levels, size of business, size of team, functions, industry, etc.

PART 2

EDGE Team Coaching with Advantycs®

CHAPTER 5

Using Advantycs® for successful EDGE Team Coaching

In this chapter we explore:

- What Advantycs® is
- The Edge Dynamics of High-Performing Teams
- Why teams are like diamonds
- The principles of diagnosing a team against the Edge Dynamics
- How the Edge Dynamics interact with each other
- Introducing a case study team and their context

About Advantycs®

When we first started thinking about high performance, we found there were over 5,000 research papers on teams, all with different perspectives. So, we decided to narrow down our focus to what was critical for the success of a high-performing team, not just any team. What gives a high-performing team an edge? We wanted to differentiate between a good and a high-performing team. From this, we distilled the research into the critical factors of high-performing teams. Advantycs® is the resulting methodology and comprises five elements:

1. The Edge Dynamics of High-Performing Teams – the conditions for high performance in a team
2. The Seven Principles of EDGE Team Coaching – the principles that underpin a high-performing team
3. The EDGE Team Coaching Process – a four-step team coaching process
4. The Team Diagnostic Tool – a tool which will help the team to assess themselves against the Edge Dynamics
5. The EDGE Team Coaching Toolkit – a set of team coaching tools for each of the Edge Dynamics

Advantycs® is simple without being simplistic. A practical, comprehensive, fully integrated, intuitive methodology for you to use as a foundation for your team coaching practice, you can use it to coach teams to fulfil their potential. Apply all of these elements in your team coaching practice to elevate the impact you have as a team coach.

We discuss the Seven Principles of EDGE Team Coaching in Chapter 6 and the EDGE Team Coaching Process in Chapter 7. We will look at an overview of the Edge Dynamics of High-Performing Teams together with the Team Diagnostic tool in this chapter; Chapters 8–12 go into each of the Edge Dynamics in more depth and reference tools for each Edge Dynamic which you can use in your team coaching practice.

The Edge Dynamics of High-Performing Teams

The Edge Dynamics are: Reason, Results, Routines, Relationships and Resilience. Together these Edge Dynamics interact and support each other to create a sustainable high-performing team.

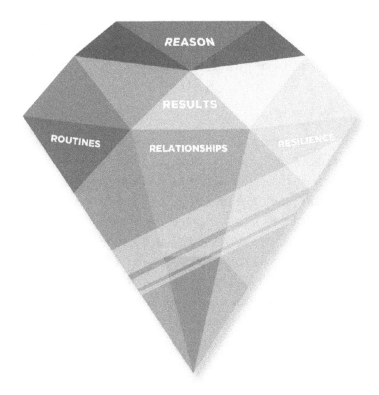

Reason is the team's *why*. Without it the team has no purpose – nothing to guide it towards where it needs to go. Results are *what* the team is accountable for delivering together. Without this, there can be duplication of effort and at best mediocre performance with an individual focus in a team. Routines are the team's ways of working, its rhythms, how the team keeps each other informed and makes decisions. Relationships are what it feels like to be a part of the team and how team members work with and interact with each other. Resilience is the energy levels of the team, learning from experiences to continuously improve and reviewing and refreshing all the Edge Dynamics regularly to anticipate and respond to changes. Routines, Relationships and Resilience together create *how* the team is going to achieve all of this. Each of these Edge Dynamics is essential – without one it is impossible to fulfil the potential of the other Edge Dynamics, which means that high performance is unlikely to be achieved and very difficult to sustain.

Work on all of the Edge Dynamics

Through our extensive work with teams, we found that many of them have previously worked on one or two of the Edge Dynamics such as Relationships or Routines and yet they were missing the most important piece of the puzzle, which is that a team needs to work on all of the Edge Dynamics to get to high performance. A team will definitely improve their performance by working on one or two Edge Dynamics, but to really get to that high performance and to sustain it over time they need to harness all of the Edge Dynamics *together*. This is because they work in an integrated way, supporting each other.

The diamond analogy

We use the analogy of a diamond when we talk about high-performing teams. We all know how special and valuable a diamond is and when we talk to teams they know implicitly how special and valuable a high-performing team is. Diamonds are multi-faceted – when you look at them, they look different depending on the angle and context that they're in. Teams also change depending on their context and are made up of different people which also makes them multi-faceted. High-performance, like a diamond, is hard to find and once a team has it, they will want to maintain it and sustain that high performance and the value that it brings them and their organization. It takes a long time to mine, cut and polish a diamond, and to fulfil the potential value of the diamond you need to go through the full process. A high-performing team takes time and effort to form, develop and sustain to fulfil its potential. The team needs to establish strong foundations in all of the Edge Dynamics to make this happen. The *why*, *what* and *how* need to be established and revisited regularly to polish their diamond. A diamond is the strongest natural material, used on the tips of drills to cut through pretty much anything. A high-performing team should be like a diamond: resilient and focused enough to cut through anything together.

Diagnosing the team

One of the most challenging aspects of team coaching is knowing what progress the team has made on their journey towards high performance. Teams are complex systems and there are so many different areas that they could work on. But how do you know where to start and what will make the difference for the team right now? You could of course ask them, but often, in our experience, teams don't really know where to start. Or they might focus on the arbitrary or easy to do.

The only way to really know where to focus is to do some kind of diagnostic of the team against the Edge Dynamics of High-Performing Teams. In individual coaching you might use assessments or diagnostic tools to help identify blind spots, build self-awareness and prioritize focus areas for your coachee. In team coaching the same principle applies. So, we've created a diagnostic tool to help you with this (see the section 'Accessing the diagnostic tool' later in this chapter). The tool will help the team identify where they will get the greatest value from their efforts and which Dynamic/s will give them the best return on their investment in moving towards high performance.

Why bother diagnosing a team?

So why bother diagnosing a team? Well, there are compelling reasons for doing a regular diagnostic. A diagnostic helps to make something that's rather subjective (in other words, how it feels to be a part of the team) into something much more tangible and data driven. Without a diagnostic, you are working with people's opinions and the danger is that the loudest voice in the room is the one that is heard while other voices get silenced. It can be hard to establish what the team as a whole really thinks. Using a research-based, anonymous diagnostic which is linked to what really impacts performance as a team enables them to prioritize and be confident that what they are working on will deliver and support them in achieving their objectives.

Regular diagnostics are key

Once the team has taken some action, we would suggest that they use their chosen diagnostic tool regularly to measure and review progress. As already mentioned, it takes ongoing practice to get to high performance and sustain it. The team is constantly shifting and adjusting. Regular diagnostics will help the team notice this. They also help the team celebrate successes, see their progress against the Edge Dynamics and diagnose and identify what to focus on next.

The first diagnostic

The first diagnostic that the team completes do will give you a baseline for the team. Where is the team right now against each of the Edge Dynamics and what should the priority be for it? Diagnosing the team helps it to prioritize the action that it should take in developing towards high performance. There are lots of factors which contribute to high performance in teams and every team is different, so knowing where to start is crucial, otherwise the team can get overwhelmed very easily and achieve very little.

How often?

We would recommend using a diagnostic tool with a team roughly every three months. This is a good rhythm to create to check in with the team on how things are going against the Edge Dynamics. It also keeps pace with any changes and shifts that are going on in the general context. Later on, once you've exited from the process, the team can continue to run their own diagnostics in some way, a great sustainable practice. Ultimately, however, the team is in charge of the timing of diagnostics.

Accessing the diagnostic tool

There are two options for carrying out a diagnostic which measures the Edge Dynamics.

1) Comprehensive diagnostic assessment for the team

The first option is to buy a subscription to our cloud-based, research-powered solution, Advantycs®, which you can learn more about on our website.[28] This solution enables the leader and the team to provide their assessment of the team against 25 questions and Stop, Start, Continue comments. The results are presented against each of the Edge Dynamics in a downloadable report. The assessment is anonymous for the team members to complete and the leader's responses are visible. The team can then discuss and use the results to take action and track their progress over time.

---

[28] www.management-dynamics.com/teamcoachingedge

2) Diagnostic coaching questions

The second option is to carry out a more informal diagnosis using the coaching questions you will find below. There are a couple of different ways you could use them.

First of all, spend some time considering the questions with the leader. What are their responses to these questions? Where are the gaps and what is the priority for them?

Secondly (and always our preference) would be to discuss the diagnostic coaching questions with the team. This gets the full team involved in diagnosing their current status as a team and creates buy in for the process from them, which, as we've already established, is crucial.

The questions are:

Reason	How clear is the team on their Reason?
	How do team members articulate the team's Reason to others?
Results	What Results are the team accountable for delivering?
	How clear is the team on the team members' accountabilities?
Routines	How well do the team's Routines serve it right now?
	Who makes most of the decisions in the team?
Relationships	What are Relationships like in the team?
	To what extent is constructive challenge a habit in the team?
Resilience	How does the team anticipate changes that affect the team?
	How are the team members' energy levels right now?

How the Edge Dynamics interact with each other

It is worth spending some time exploring how the Edge Dynamics interact with each other and there is no strong set process for how to engage with them. Consider what the team needs right now in your coaching process.

Where do you start?

People often ask us 'where do you start when coaching a team? Which Edge Dynamic has priority?' There is a broad sequence and a rule of thumb to follow when coaching a team which is: start with Reason – coach the team to understand their *why*; then coach them to gain clarity on the team's Results and then explore the *how*, including the Routines, Relationships and Resilience in the team.

However, the reality is that *all* of the Edge Dynamics are deeply interconnected with each other. Edge Dynamics are levers the team can pull for an impact, and by focusing on one Edge Dynamic they will naturally, by extension, impact other Edge Dynamics at the same time.

Lack of connection to Reason

What we've noticed, working with hundreds of teams, is that if a team is overworked it can be easy to lose sight of their Reason. Reminding teams of and reconnecting them to their Reason – their *why* – can really help them to focus and re-energize to move forward.

Lack of focus on Results

If Results are poor in a team, no matter how great the Reason, Routines, Relationships or Resilience are, the team will be considered by their key stakeholders to be failing. A team's success is determined by the Results they deliver according to the rest of the organization.

Ineffective Routines

If Routines are poor in a team, it can affect all the other Edge Dynamics. It can cause low productivity, duplication of effort and over-collaboration, which will impact Relationships. Resilience will be impacted because people will feel over-worked and the links of their Results to the team Reason will be unclear.

Poor Relationships

We've also noticed that if Relationships aren't working in a team, then it's really hard to deliver on Results in that team – the team gets distracted by conflict, opinions and ideas are not shared and poor decisions are made. If a team's Routines are out of date or cumbersome, this can damage both the Relationships within the team and their ability to deliver on Results. It also leaves the team feeling demotivated and disengaged, which impacts Resilience.

When Relationships are poor in a team we often find certain team members can be excluded from the team process; for example, in a team meeting, their opinions are shut down or they're not invited to share their opinions in the first place. This will impact Relationships within the team and also the Results that that team can potentially achieve. Results will be limited by the lack of diversity of thought, debate and challenge within the team. The team may also be a victim of 'group think'.

Low Resilience

When Resilience is low in a team, getting clarity on the Reason and the Results impacts their Resilience as they are not able to see the wood for the trees, to be able to prioritize and to focus on building Relationships within the team to get stuff done.

Ultimately, it doesn't really matter where you start. What is more important is actually starting and getting the team's buy in to doing so. Coach the team to decide where they would like to start first and which Edge Dynamics would make the most sense for them right now. While coaching a team, continuously use the Edge Dynamics and the diagnostic to raise the team's awareness of the dynamics within the team and how they impact each other.

Case study team

We have worked with hundreds of teams over many decades and have condensed a typical experience of team coaching into this case study to highlight the challenges and issues teams often face and how team coaching can support them to achieve high performance. It's a fictional team, but the issues, approaches and results are real. In Chapters 8–12 we will come back to this case study team again as we explore each Edge Dynamic from their perspective.

Context

The team are a global leadership team, led by Michaela Janus. There are 10 team members, including the leader, most of whom are based in Amsterdam. Michaela joined the business three months ago as

CEO and the rest of the team has been pretty well established for about 18 months with the exception of John Fisher, the CFO who Michaela brought with her from her last company and who joined soon after she did.

The team coaching approach

The first step was to meet with the leader to discuss what team coaching is and isn't and how it is different from other team development activities she may have come across before. We asked questions to understand the context that the team is operating in, the opportunities as she sees them and the challenges they need to overcome. We discussed what her view of success is and what process she would like to follow with the team. We agreed to use the Advantycs® diagnostic tool, with the intention of working with the team for 12 months and having a series of workshops and 'coaching moments' throughout the process. Success would be measured via the diagnostic tool and others measures as defined with the team in the first session. We agreed how we would work with her and the team.

The leader's view of the team

Michaela is very optimistic about both the business and the team. She thinks the team members are all good, strong individuals that will add a lot of value to the organization, they're just not there yet as a team. She sees evidence that they lead their own respective teams well, although there is room for improvement in places.

The opportunity for the team

The team are operating as a pretty siloed group of individuals and the sense of a real team which is leading the business together is missing. Day to day, team members are more interested in the teams that they each respectively lead than the leadership team. Some of them lead enormous teams of thousands of people and generate large amounts of revenue for the organization (e.g. General Managers). Others have smaller functions with deep expertise that work across the organization. The big opportunity for this team is for them to shift their mindset from 'me' to 'we' – to really tap into the potential that a high-performing team has to take the business to the next level. The competitive landscape is changing, with new technologies entering the marketplace, making it a complex environment with unprecedented challenges. In order to succeed, the team will need to lead the organisation, adapt fast and collaborate.

The first diagnostic

Having briefed the team, we invited each team member to complete an initial diagnostic of the team using the Advantycs® diagnostic tool. The results were, as expected, mixed, showing an OK team with huge potential for improvement. There was a very wide range of responses, with the lowest scoring individual reporting across all 25 questions an average of 1.8 out of 5 and the highest scoring individual reporting a whopping 4.2. A range this large suggests a huge variation in experience of the team members.

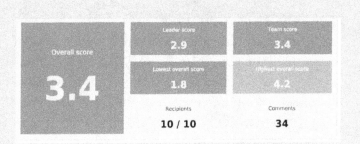

The highest scoring Edge Dynamic was Reason with a very respectable 4.1 overall. Relationships were moderate with 3.5 and the other Edge Dynamics were low, ranging from 2.7 to 3.3. Resilience scored the lowest of all the Edge Dynamics with 2.7, which is very weak.

The first session with the team

In the first session, we contracted with the team about the approach to their team coaching, discussing confidentiality and what team coaching is and isn't. We ran the Defining High Performance Exercise[29] with the team which helped them to articulate where they are now and what their desired outcome is in 12

---

[29] Download from www.management-dynamics.com/teamcoachingedge

months' time. We reviewed the Advantycs® diagnostic results with the team and they discussed the insights it gave them about their team dynamics. They then identified their priorities and some measures of success for the team coaching, which included a target Advantycs® overall score – they wanted all Edge Dynamics to be in the green within 12 months.

Using Advantycs® for Successful Team Coaching – a summary

You won't coach a team to high performance overnight. It takes deliberate action by the whole team and takes time. The Edge Dynamics of High-Performing Teams are:

- Reason
- Results
- Routines
- Relationships
- Resilience

Reason is *why* the team exists, its purpose beyond delivering KPIs

Results are *what* the team is accountable for delivering

Routines, Relationships and Resilience are *how* the team operates

All of the Edge Dynamics interact with and impact each other so coach the team to pay attention to and work on all of them to achieve high performance. Use a diagnostic tool like Advantycs® regularly to determine how the team is doing against each of the Edge Dynamics and build their skill in sustaining their review of them long term.

CHAPTER 6

The Seven Principles of EDGE Team Coaching

In this chapter we explore:

- The Seven Principles of EDGE Team Coaching

When working with a team, it can be helpful to have a set of principles in mind, principles which when they are all present will ultimately lead to their increased performance. These principles will be a map for your team coaching and cut across all the Edge Dynamics. We have identified seven key principles in our team coaching practice to keep in mind whenever you work with a team. The seven principles are:

1. Develop the dynamics within the team
2. Create an inclusive culture
3. Increase interdependence
4. Build a sense of untapped potential
5. Celebrate similarities and differences
6. Take a systemic view of the team
7. Sustain high performance

1. Develop the dynamics within the team

High performance can only be achieved and sustained long term when the team consistently reviews their dynamics. They should take a systemic perspective and continuously adjust and adapt to changing context, strategy, workload and team members. The Edge Dynamics of Reason, Results, Routines, Relationships and Resilience (see Chapters 8–12 for more information) are the key to this. If a team regularly reviews all of these Edge Dynamics, they will maximize their chances of being high performing.

When a team has poor dynamics they will:

- Have frustration caused by lack of clarity, conflict or many other things
- Feel either bored or over-worked
- Feel undervalued and lost in the organization
- Focus on their individual work, potentially being territorial with other team members

When a team has great team dynamics they will:

- Have high levels of engagement
- Be able to sustain high performance
- Continuously learn and grow together
- Truly appreciate the benefits that the team gives them as individuals

Teams sometimes (quite often!) prioritize the achievement of a task or goal over the dynamics within the team. They would say that delivery of results comes first and the dynamics are nice to have. However, as we've established in Chapter 2 when we talk about what high performance is in a team, both the achievement of objectives and the dynamics in the team need to be optimized in order to sustain high performance long term. Teams need to invest in great Routines to review the Edge Dynamics regularly and then adjust their approach accordingly. Achievement of objectives will naturally follow in a self-sustaining manner.

To coach a team to develop their dynamics, create buy in from the team by sharing the Edge Dynamics with them and the definition of high performance in teams. Get them to consider what high performance could be for them and how the Edge Dynamics will support this. Use a diagnostic regularly (see Chapter 5) to help them turn something which is quite subjective (how it feels to be a part of this team right now) into something a bit more concrete and objective. Use the diagnostic as a vehicle for reflection and discussion about the Edge Dynamics. Where appropriate bring observations about the Edge Dynamics to the team's attention, thereby holding up the mirror to blind spots they might not yet have noticed.

2. Create an inclusive culture

Research shows how important inclusion is in high-performing teams.[30] Teams can achieve inclusion by creating a common identity and then ensuring that every team member is treated with respect, regardless of their background or personality. Inclusion is an essential part of a high-performing team, and this means that in the key moments when a team of people work together on something, they include everyone in the process and everyone's contribution is respected and valued. This doesn't mean that everyone works together on everything all the time, nor does it mean consensus needs to be reached on every decision. Indicators of poor inclusive culture include:

- Team members focus on themselves first, asserting their ideas without including others proactively in the process
- Communication in the team is primarily with the leader rather than with each other

---

[30] https://learning.linkedin.com/resources/learning-culture/diversity-workplace-statistics-dei-importance

- They will share frustrations about the team to others outside of the team
- Cliques exist in the team

When a team has high levels of inclusion, they:

- Take accountability for resolving poor dynamics in the team themselves
- Communicate with each other as well as with the leader
- Share frustrations and solve issues together
- Are proactively inclusive of others in the team, inviting them into conversations and debates

When all of this happens, it's noticeable both within and outside of the team. External stakeholders will comment positively on the team's positive culture.

The team should use inclusion deliberately in the moments that matter such as strategic discussions and important decision-making. Coach the team to pay attention to the quieter members of the team and invite them into the conversation. Coach the leader to ensure that team contributions (such as organization of social events, leading key projects) are spread equally throughout the team and that they don't default to the same person each time. Teams can share the role of chair of meetings to improve inclusion, which means that each team meeting is led by a different team member rather than just the leader of the team.

To coach a team to create an inclusive culture, when you are contracting with the leader and team, think about how to ensure that they demonstrate inclusive behaviours and are all committed to being coached as a single entity. If team members contact you outside of the coaching process, bear in mind the need for them to be inclusive in your response. For example, having side conversations about the team with a team member undermines this idea. Encourage the team member to bring their thoughts or concerns to either the next team session or a team meeting, or to the leader if they don't feel psychologically safe to do so in a team context.

3. Increase interdependence

Many teams complain of working in siloes. They recognize that in order to be truly high performing they need better collaboration, otherwise they will only compete with each other. The true value of a team can only be realized when there is a certain level of interdependence, when team members work together on critical tasks to achieve their objectives. When teams need to solve complex problems, interdependence is the key. Understanding this and enhancing their interdependence is critical for their success. Most humans enjoy working with others at least some of the time and so while interdependence creates better collaboration, it also builds a sense of belonging, common identity and Resilience. Teams should consider not only the interdependencies within the team itself but also others within the system of which they are a part.

When a team has low levels of interdependence they will:

- Work in siloes, independently of each other and key stakeholders
- Only talk about their own personal objectives, not those of the team
- Compete with each other for team resources
- Not be particularly interested in each other's work

When a team has high levels of interdependence they will:

- Work together on key tasks which add value to them and the team
- Be willing to share resources
- Discuss team objectives as well as how to support each other's personal objectives
- Be motivated to collaborate because they rely on each other to deliver results

The larger a team is the harder it is to create high levels of interdependence across the whole team. Forcing people to work together just for the sake of it creates over-collaboration and frustration, so be careful of coaching a team to work on everything together all the time. Coach them to be selective and intentional about when interdependence would be valuable and when working independently is more effective.

In larger teams, coach the team to assign delegations – in other words, subsets of the team who will work on a task together and then report back to the wider team for information, input and decision-making. This requires absolute clarity on the scope of the task, deadlines and the role of the rest of the team in the process. It also requires the right people to be in the delegation from the beginning, or consulted with at the right time during the process.

Sharing objectives within a team fosters interdependence by aligning individual efforts with collective goals. When team members openly communicate their objectives and aspirations, this transparency encourages collaboration. As individuals recognize the interplay of their roles in achieving the team's goals, they are more likely to support one another, pool their resources and coordinate their actions effectively. This interdependence not only enhances team cohesion but also promotes a sense of responsibility and mutual accountability. In essence, shared objectives create a web of interconnectivity that strengthens team dynamics and bolsters their ability to tackle challenges and achieve success together.

4. Build a sense of untapped potential

Teams need to buy into and be excited about the team coaching process. In order to do this, they have to believe that more is possible and that the team will be greater than the sum of its parts. They need to feel like there is untapped potential in the team and a benefit to them personally from working together. This will motivate them to engage in the team coaching and maintain that effort over time.

When a team has a low sense of untapped potential, they:

- Feel overwhelmed by the perception of the effort required to get to high performance
- Can't conceive of how developing the team will benefit them personally
- Might express cynicism about team development
- Are reluctant to dedicate their time or energy to developing the team

When a team has a high sense of untapped potential, they:

- Get excited about the possibilities of what developing the team could bring
- Can easily step into the future and imagine the team achieving high performance
- Exude confidence that it's worth putting the effort in
- Are willing to give time and energy to developing the team

To coach a team to build their sense of untapped potential, you could start by helping them to identify with high-performing teams – by thinking about high-performing teams they know of (which could be sports teams or a team they have been part of in the past). Then help them to step into the future of their own team by imagining what high performance would look like for this team. We often do a 'see, say, feel' exercise with teams to achieve this – what would they see, what would they say and what would they feel when they have high performance? This lights up the team with an idea of that future being possible using three of the major senses.

It could be useful, in a particularly resistant team, to run an exercise where they articulate individually the benefits to themselves as individual team members of a high-performing team. Get each team member to share their insight with the wider group. This creates buy in for the idea of untapped potential and develops it even further for each team member.

Coach the team to overcome any objections they might have about the future state of the team. Bring these objections into the conversation by asking questions like:

- What will get in the way of you achieving your potential as a team?
- What's bothering you about the idea of high performance?

These will bring the objections into the room, where other team members can overcome them through the conversation and your coaching process. One that pops up a lot is the fear of the additional effort required to achieve high performance. This stops them even perceiving what the team's potential is. Talking about this and reframing the conversation to be about working smarter, not harder can be useful.

5. Celebrate similarities and differences

Similarities and differences are both really important in teams – they are the lifeblood of a high-performing team. We naturally need a sense of similarity to build the trust and psychological safety that's so essential in a team. We need to perceive that people are like us in some, even small, way to develop sufficient levels of trust. However, differences are equally important because they are the root of innovation, problem-solving and expanding team perspectives. Without difference we don't experience the diversity of thought that is necessary to make superior decisions and identify more effective ways of working. If we only have similarity, we get 'group think', 'stuckness' and the status quo.

When a team doesn't celebrate similarities and differences, they:

- Struggle to articulate what their similarities and differences are
- Rely on their similarities to get things done
- Get frustrated by the differences in the team
- Don't flex their behaviour to work more effectively with others in the team

When a team celebrates similarities and differences, they:

- Know what their similarities and differences are
- Utilize both their similarities and their differences to make better decisions
- Seek to overcome frustration with differences and use it positively
- Flex their behaviours to work more effectively with others in the team

Coaching a team to notice and value the similarities in the team can be really valuable. Use team exercises which highlight team members, similarities, without creating a 'clone' culture. We like the values exercise,[31] for example, which invariably demonstrates the similarities in what team members think is important at work. Even when team members have different values at first glance, when they dig deeper, the similarities and resonances are there.

When contracting with the team, and they establish the expectations they have of each other, encourage them to notice the foundation for differences to be shared respectfully. Difference is about diversity of thought, encouraging different perspectives and approaches to a task. It's about enabling people to be their whole self in a team and about enabling people to broaden how they think about the world. Coach the team to practice curiosity and to value differences for the benefits they bring to the team.

6. Take a systemic view of the team

A team doesn't operate in isolation. They are part of a system, with key stakeholders, clients, suppliers and other influences. Teams need to broaden their perspectives to include all of these aspects in order to be truly high performing. Once they understand the different influences and their impact on the team, the team can make decisions about how they can influence those parts of the system. High-performing teams look at themselves from multiple viewpoints – they take an outside in as well as inside out approach. They put themselves in their stakeholders' shoes and think about what high performance means to them.

---

[31] See www.management-dynamics.com/teamcoachingedge for more details.

When a team has a narrow view of the team, they:

- Focus solely on the internal team dynamics
- Talk about 'us and them' in relation to their stakeholders
- Don't see how they impact the wider organization
- Feel misunderstood by others in the organization

When a team takes a systemic view of the team, they:

- Focus on all their stakeholders as a system
- Feel empowered to influence the wider system they are a part of
- Are clear about their impact and value in the wider organization
- Engage with their stakeholders to increase understanding and make a difference

The team could take a systemic view by creating a systemic map. This maps the team members, their key stakeholders and other elements (such as the organizational strategy, the team's key customer or the economy) in relation to each other. Coach the team to consider each of those relationships and their nature. Look at the current state and then map the desired future state. This exercise is an excellent way for the team to take a systemic view of their context and to gain insights on how to impact the system.

The team could bring the systemic perspective into strategic discussions and decision-making by stepping into the shoes of their key stakeholders and then viewing the discussion or decision through their eyes. This can be a very powerful practice for understanding the situation from different angles and coming up with a more innovative solution. It also helps teams to appreciate their stakeholders' worlds and the pressure they experience.

7. Sustain high performance

High-performing teams don't just achieve high performance, they sustain it over time without ongoing support from a team coach. Some teams will achieve high performance for a short period of time by accident or luck, but no team can sustain high performance for a long period of time without intentionally taking action to fulfil the Edge Dynamics.

When a team is not sustaining high performance, they:

- Have high levels of burnout or turnover in the team
- Demonstrate inconsistent performance, sometimes achieving their KPIs, other times missing them
- Make mistakes and repeat them
- Rely on the leader, team coach or other external parties to help them with their performance

When a team is sustaining high performance, they:

- Are resilient and are able to re-energize themselves
- Consistently achieve their KPIs
- Learn from their mistakes and celebrate successes
- Have self-managing practices for high performance

The team could create Routines which build a rhythm of reflecting on the Edge Dynamics in the team and taking regular, continuous action to improve. These Routines should form part of their natural cadence of meetings and interactions as a team. They should not in the long term rely on sessions with you as a team coach or anyone else.

Challenges occur in teams, the key to a high-performing team is to have the foundation in place to be able to deal with them when they happen. The team should have Routines in place to anticipate challenges, but also rehearse the team's response to unanticipated challenges. When these happen, who will make decisions? How will workload be managed? How will team members support each other in their Resilience? How will you learn from the experience?

Coaching for high performance – a summary

We have identified seven key principles in our team coaching practice. Have all of these principles in mind whenever you work with a team and consistently strive to coach the team to develop them:

1. Develop the dynamics within the team

High-performance teams prioritize reviewing and adjusting their Edge Dynamics, including Reason, Results, Routines, Relationships and Resilience. Neglected dynamics lead to frustration, imbalances and individualism, while strong dynamics yield engagement and sustained high performance. Teams should balance objectives and dynamics for lasting success through regular review.

2. Create an inclusive culture

Inclusion is vital for high-performing teams, where everyone's input is respected. Poor inclusion is marked by self-centredness, limited communication, venting outside the team and cliques. High inclusion involves accountability, open communication, collective problem-solving and external recognition. Coaching should promote inclusion in key moments.

3. Increase interdependence

Effective teams need interdependence to collaborate on crucial tasks, share resources and align personal and team objectives. Low interdependence results in isolation and competition, while high interdependence leads to collaborative, resource-sharing and goal-focused teams. Tailor the level of interdependence to the team's complexity and size, avoiding over-collaboration.

4. Build a sense of untapped potential

Teams must be motivated and believe in their untapped potential to engage in team coaching effectively. A low sense of potential leads to overwhelm and reluctance, while a high sense of potential generates excitement and confidence. Help the team to envision high performance, address objections and reframe the conversation to focus on working smarter, not harder.

5. Celebrate similarities and differences

Teams benefit from both similarities and differences. Similarities create trust and safety, while differences drive innovation and diverse perspectives. Teams that embrace both can make better decisions and adapt effectively, while those that don't struggle and may fall into 'group think'. Encourage the team to value both aspects, using exercises to highlight similarities and establishing expectations that promote respectful differences and diverse thinking.

6. Take a systemic view of the team

High-performing teams recognize their connection to a larger system with stakeholders and external influences. They broaden their perspective and make informed decisions by understanding their impact on the entire system. They engage with stakeholders and use tools like systemic maps to gain insights and develop innovative solutions.

7. Sustain high performance

Sustaining high team performance requires intentional effort and focus on the Edge Dynamics. When teams neglect this, they face burnout, inconsistency and external reliance, while successful teams remain resilient, meet their KPIs consistently and develop self-managing practices. To maintain high performance, teams should establish routines for reflection and anticipate and prepare for challenges, ensuring a solid foundation for decision-making, workload management and team support.

CHAPTER 7

The EDGE Team Coaching Process

In this chapter we explore:

- Having a process for team coaching
- Understanding who the client is
- Considering whether the team is coachable or not

Have a process for team coaching

In individual coaching there are many models, (such as GROW,[32] OSCAR[33] and CLEAR[34]) which are applicable to individual as well as team coaching situations. For the team coaching scenario we believe it is important to broaden your perspective in your team coaching practice, so we developed our own four-step process called The EDGE Team Coaching Process.

---

[32] John Whitmore, *Coaching for performance, the principles and practice of coaching and leadership* (2017).

[33] Andrew Gilbert and Karen Whittleworth, *OSCAR coaching model: Simplifying workplace coaching* (2009).

[34] Peter Hawkins, *Creating a coaching culture* (2012).

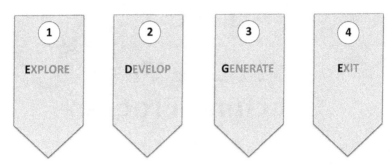

The EDGE team coaching process

Step 1: Explore

The first step in a team coaching process is to explore what is going on for the team. Start by meeting with the leader and (if required) their key stakeholders. Ask them the following questions:

- What is the team's situation and context in the wider organization?
- What is the team and organizational culture?
- What are the drivers of a team coaching process for this team?
- Why team coaching now?
- How engaged are the team in the process?
- Who's initiated the process?
- What changes do they hope to see out of the team coaching process?
- What does high performance look like for them?
- What challenges do they anticipate in the process?
- Who needs to be informed or involved in the process?
- What are the financial and time constraints?
- Who are the team members? Tell me about them.
- What are the dynamics like in the team? What would they like to change about that?

- Do any of the team members work in a matrix environment (where they have dotted line reporting into another part of the business)? What impact does this have on the team dynamics?
- What will the team need to unlearn in order to be high performing?

At this stage you can get an insight into the performance of the team – to what extent are they achieving their KPIs? What are they? How does the wider business assess the team's performance? You might use various sources for this such as engagement surveys, feedback from key stakeholders and their own reporting on KPIs.

Ideally meet with the whole team early on in the process for introductions and to establish credibility and rapport. It may also be appropriate, with permission from the leader, to meet with the team's key stakeholders to get their views on the strengths and development areas for the team.

Understand who the client is

In individual coaching it's usually fairly obvious that your client is the coachee. However, in team coaching, it's more complex as there are many stakeholders to consider. Your primary client is the team as a single entity. This includes the leader and the team members together. Often it will feel like the leader is the primary client as they are usually the one you have the greatest interaction with and who may have engaged you. However, think of your client as the whole team and your team coaching will be much more effective and you will be more able to maintain the objectivity and trust needed to coach the team effectively.

But who's the client if the leader and team haven't engaged you for the team coaching? Perhaps the engagement has come from the HR team, who have identified that a team needs some team coaching support. It's still the team as a single entity. You just have an additional stakeholder you will need to consider and manage.

When team coaching, you need a multi-layered approach to contracting with stakeholders – discuss with each stakeholder:

- Confidentiality – what will you share with them and what won't you share? For example, we often contract with stakeholders outside of the team that we won't share individual comments from team coaching sessions and we will only share the outputs of team coaching sessions with agreement from the team. We may share themes across teams, again with the knowledge of the team. Ideally, the team will share these outputs directly with the stakeholders themselves.
- Desired outcomes – the team may have different desired outcomes than other external stakeholders. It may be useful to bring in other stakeholders to agree desired outcomes at the start, but again do this with the team's permission. You may encourage the team to engage with their stakeholders themselves as an action after a team coaching session.

Is team coaching right for this team?

In the Explore stage of the process, while you are seeking to understand the context for the team, have one eye continuously on whether team coaching is the right solution at this time for the team. Team coaching is not always the right approach for every team, nor may they be willing to invest in the process.

Watch out for the following indicators, which suggest that team coaching might not be the right approach for a team:

- They are looking for a quick fix or a 'tick box' exercise
- They just want to have fun together and 'not get too serious'
- They don't want to invest the time needed to be successful at team coaching
- They are looking for skills development
- The leader is not fully invested in the team coaching process (they want a 'do to the team' process)
- The team doesn't see the point in changing their dynamics

If these indicators are present, consider what other team development approaches may be more appropriate for the team right now.

Using a diagnostic
Using a diagnostic of some sort early on in the Explore part of the process can be invaluable, both as a tool to provide insights on where the team currently is but also as a method for measuring progress later. See Chapter 5 for details on the Advantycs® Diagnostic tool. Make sure you debrief the results of the diagnostic with the leader and the team.

Step 2: Develop

The next step is to develop your team coaching approach with the leader and their team. Partner with them to create an approach which helps the team to evoke awareness of their strengths, development areas – known and unknown (also called 'blind spots'). Successful team coaching doesn't stop here, it also gets the team to practise the behaviours they would like to see in the team as well as facilitating the growth of the team through ongoing action in between sessions. Meet with the leader to contract the overall team coaching approach and how you will work with them and the team throughout the coaching process. This part is crucial – there needs to be a beginning and an ending to your coaching. In your first session with the team, you will also need to contract with them on the following:

- What team coaching is and is not – describing the different methods that might be used in the process
- How the team and you will behave before, during and after team coaching sessions
- What the sessions will focus on
- Where accountability for results sits (i.e. with the team, not with you as coach)
- Confidentiality
- How and when you will exit from the team coaching process

Consider how you, the team and their key stakeholders will measure the success of the team coaching.

Types of teams

In our experience of working with hundreds of teams, we have observed that there are two types of team – simple and complex. Neither type is right or wrong, better or worse, it is just useful to know what type of team you are coaching. Each has their own unique set of needs and requires a different approach to applying the Edge Dynamics.

- Simple teams

We define a simple team as one where all of the team members have the same leader but very little, if any, interdependence (yet) between each other to get their jobs done. They can deliver their role independently of their colleagues within the team. They may have interdependencies outside of the team and they may do a similar role to others in the team.

Sales teams are often simple teams as they are made up of a group of salespeople all doing similar roles, maybe with different territories/accounts/verticals. Their main interface in the team is with the leader. Each of them will have relationships and interdependencies outside of the team such as the product manager, the customer service team or the logistics team, but have few interdependencies within the team itself. The problem with a simple team like a sales team is that it can be hard to create a feeling of 'team'.

Forcing a simple team to collaborate for the sake of collaboration is a waste of time and resources and yet we see it happening all the time. Leaders invest huge amounts of time in team building without really understanding the type of team that they have and where the greatest value is. There must be benefits to the individuals concerned as well as to the team as a whole. Simple teams, in our experience, collaborate well on sharing best practice or innovation and continuous improvement projects. They will need to be given permission to collaborate and rewarded for doing so.

- Complex teams

We define a complex team as one where there are multiple interdependencies amongst team members, who rely on others in the team to get things done. The benefit of a complex team is that they can complete complicated tasks much more effectively and realize the advantages of working together with others to solve problems. The ability to collaborate, explore different points of view and gain new perspectives enables a team to be innovative. In fact, research shows that a group of people will make a better decision than one person alone.[35]

---

[35] www.forbes.com/sites/eriklarson/2017/09/21/new-research-diversity-inclusion-better-decision-making-at-work/?sh=5142d8704cbf

Interdependence creates complexity because of the number of relationships and touchpoints that are required to be successful between team members. We are talking about human beings here and people are wonderfully different and complex in their own right. It's easy for misunderstandings and conflict to occur between people. It's also common for people to be misaligned as to how the work gets done without investing time in discussions and agreements. Therefore, a complex team needs more support in setting themselves up for success. This is where team coaching can add the most value.

Complex teams are also complex because they change constantly. New people join, people leave and the context in which they operate changes around them. This means that the team continuously needs to adapt and evolve to sustain high performance. A complex team is never 'done' when it comes to high performance.

A risk in a complex team is over-collaboration. It's easy to over-complicate processes and interdependencies. Collaboration needs to add value to everyone while at the same time increasing productivity.

Leadership teams are always, by default, complex teams. However, not all leadership teams operate as if they are a complex team and might act as if they are a simple team instead. You can see how this might happen – a leadership team usually comprises of heads of functions who have their own large functional teams below them in the organizational hierarchy. They may come together as a leadership team only once a month (or whatever rhythm the team has established) whereas they are operating with their functional teams on a daily basis. Their personal credibility is primarily about their functional area of responsibility. The organization and wider system rewards them for the success of their own function. The emphasis, therefore, quite naturally, is the team they lead rather than the leadership team they are a part of. If this is happening at the leadership team level, you can guarantee it is mirrored further down the organization. As complex teams, leadership teams should be capitalizing on their untapped potential to create true high performance. And as a leadership team, the benefits for the whole organization are massive. This is where the competitive edge will be realized.

Team size

As with many things in life, when it comes to a team, size does matter. The optimal size of a team will depend on whether it is simple or complex. Simple teams can be much larger and still be effective. The main impact of a large team here is the leader's capacity to manage all of their team members independently. We regularly see simple teams of 20–25 people.

Complex teams need to be much smaller – but not too small – to enable team members to effectively manage all of the Relationships they need. Here, collaboration is key, but it takes time and if too many people are involved, you risk over-collaboration and inefficiency. According to McKinsey, a leadership team comprising less than six people 'is likely to result in poorer decisions because of a lack of diversity, and slower decision making because of a lack of bandwidth. Research also suggests that the team's effectiveness starts to diminish if there are more than ten people on it. Sub-teams start to form, encouraging divisive behaviour'. [36]

As we've discussed already in Chapter 6, a high-performing team is one where there is an inclusive culture. The bigger the team, the harder it becomes to ensure everyone is

---

[36] www.mckinsey.com/business-functions/people-and-organizational-performance/our-insights/high-performing-teams-a-timeless-leadership-topic

heard and included. Inclusive meetings will take longer when they have more people. It then becomes essential for the leader to learn strong facilitation techniques which will help speed up decision-making without undermining the quality of the conversation and the sharing of ideas and thoughts.

The bigger the team, the easier it is for cliques or sub-groups to form. Human beings naturally form groups, even within a team, and they will happen along the lines of who has common interests, backgrounds, experiences. Cliques are by their nature excluding and should be avoided if the team wants to be high performing. The team should spend time building Relationships with people they have less in common with naturally. If cliques appear in the team, what is encouraging this? Does the leader, for example, spend more time with some people in their team than with others? This can create a perception of favourites which will hinder team cohesion and therefore performance.

• Coaching a small, simple team

This can be the most straightforward type of team to coach. With this type of team, in our experience, it is about creating a common identity which is sufficient to create community and loyalty. It's also about building a sense of untapped potential, helping them to realize that when they work together there are benefits to each team member such as support and solidarity. While the team's tasks have minimal opportunities for interdependence, the benefits of collaboration can still be achieved through team members working on improving common systems and processes or best practices.

• Coaching a large, simple team

When you're coaching a large, simple team it can be harder to develop a sense of common identity as you're dealing with more people and their opinions. It's harder for them to reach consensus on things. Team sessions take longer because there are more people in the team. Manage the expectations of the sponsor about what is possible to achieve with a team like this. Consider breaking the team into sub-groups at certain points to work on things on behalf of the whole team. Working with a co-coach in large teams is highly recommended.

• Coaching a small, complex team

When you're coaching a small, complex team, bear in mind all of the principles we discussed in Chapter 6. Their smaller size can make achieving the principles easier and therefore quicker, so it will be about helping them to get to sustaining high performance. Coach them to create an inclusive culture, increase their interdependence to the appropriate level and build a sense of untapped potential. Help them to celebrate and utilize their similarities and differences. The smaller the team, the less difference there may be so you may need to coach them to lean into differences even more than in any other team type. Because the team size will prevent them from having broad enough perspectives, you will need to coach them to take an even broader view and consider the team from a systemic horizon.

• Coaching a large, complex team

This can be the hardest type of team to coach because they have so many interdependencies which already exist. It may be hard to create an inclusive culture because there are so many people in the team, but it will be worth it in the end. Inclusion is very hard to create just because of the impracticalities of giving everyone airtime in the team. Every team activity or team coaching conversation you run will take longer because of this! Large, complex teams are at significant risk of over-collaboration because of their size and complexity. Coach them to be discerning about where they spend their time collaboratively. It can be easier to find difference in a large, complex team because there are more people, but it's harder to find the similarities right across the team. You may need to break them into smaller groups for many activities. Work with the team to establish whether they are in fact one team or a constellation of teams interacting together. Working with a co-coach is highly recommended in large teams.

Step 3: Generate

In this stage you will be coaching the team to generate awareness and develop towards their desired outcomes. You may need to recontract with the team at various points in the process as things shift and change. In each session you run, hold them accountable for taking action back in their interactions with each other. Teams that do this will be far more successful and will make quicker, more sustainable progress than teams that don't.

Initially some teams may come back to the second session you run with them having made little or no progress on their actions. This is a great opportunity to bring this to their attention and to challenge them to consider to what extent this reflects their normal team dynamic and what got in the way of them taking the action they committed to.

If you are using a diagnostic tool, you could rerun the diagnostic periodically to track progress and help the team to prioritize targeted action.

An essential part of this stage is about supporting the leader to maintain momentum and to consider their role in leading the team to high performance. For example, they will need to think about how they role model the behaviours the team want to create, how they can get in the way of the performance of their team and what they can change in their own leadership to accelerate the team's development. We would suggest meeting with the leader separately from the rest of the team before and after each team coaching session. You can also check in with the leader during team coaching sessions to ensure they are happy with the direction the conversations are going and how you're coaching the team.

Consider whether the team is coachable or not
This is a critical factor in your success as a team coach – you will need to watch out for this continuously. If a team (or leader) is not coachable, you should not continue. Make sure you've managed their expectation and contracted on this in the Explore and Develop stages of the process.

Some indicators that they are not coachable are:

- Cancelling team coaching sessions last minute
- Attending the sessions but not really being present (on phones, laptops, popping out for meetings, etc.)
- The team, as a whole, repeatedly not following up on their actions
- Not being willing to commit to changing behaviours
- Being very passive in a team coaching session. This might show up as a reluctance to take part in team coaching activities or to discuss and explore insights
- Being extremely defensive about the status quo

You may have a couple of team members demonstrating these behaviours and that doesn't mean that the team as a whole is uncoachable. It can be frustrating for other team members, but it still possible to turn them around with the leader's support and great coaching skills. However, if you are seeing this across a majority of the team or if the leader is demonstrating these behaviours, consider whether you should proceed and bring this awareness to the team. Contracting is essential to enable you as a coach to deal with these behaviours if they pop up. Make sure you've discussed with the team what your expected behaviours are and bring them back to the team when they are not demonstrating them.

Step 4: Exit

This stage is essential and so often neglected by team coaches. We would argue it's as important as the Explore stage of the relationship. High performance is an ongoing process – and remember it happens by design – but if the team coach is creating a relationship of dependency, they are ultimately not serving the team. This stage of the team coaching process is about creating a great ending and leaving the team with strategies for developing their own routines for coaching themselves. This enables ongoing, sustained high performance. Plan your own exit with the team from the coaching process.

To end a team coaching process, build in a review process which supports the team to consider their desired outcomes and measures of success and identifies where they are now in relation to that – what progress have they made, what feels different and how should they celebrate that progress? It should also recognize that they are not (ever) done in their process to high performance and should consider what is next in that process and how they will move forward without you supporting them.

The ending of this process doesn't mean that you can't work with them ever again. It just means that you've ended this part of your work with them and can be re-engaged at some point in the future on a new coaching engagement with a new contract in place.

When following the EDGE Team Coaching Process, remember to always have in mind the team coaching principles (see Chapter 6).

The EDGE Team Coaching Process – a summary

It is important to broaden your perspective in your team coaching practice, so we developed our own four-step process for coaching teams.

1. Explore – The first step in a team coaching process is to explore what is going on for the team. Start by meeting with the leader and (if required) their key stakeholders. Ask them key questions to help your understanding of the context for the team.
2. Develop – The next step is to develop your team coaching approach with the leader and their team. Partner with them to create an approach which helps the team to evoke awareness of their strengths and development areas. Contract with the team.
3. Generate – In this stage you will be coaching the team to generate awareness and develop towards their desired outcomes. You may need to recontract with the team at various points in the process as things shift and change.
4. Exit – This stage of the team coaching process is about creating a great ending and leaving the team with strategies for creating their own routines for coaching themselves. This enables ongoing, sustained high performance. Plan your own exit with the team from the coaching process.

In individual coaching it's usually fairly obvious that your client is the coachee. However, in team coaching, it's more complex as there are many stakeholders to consider. Your primary client is the team as a single entity. This includes the leader and the team members together.

When team coaching, you need a multi-layered approach to contracting with stakeholders – discuss with each stakeholder:

1. Confidentiality
2. Desired outcomes

Knowing whether a team is coachable is a critical factor in your success as a team coach – you will need to watch out for this continuously. If a team (or leader) is not coachable, you should fire yourself as their coach and not continue.

There are two types of team:

1. Simple
2. Complex

Neither type is right or wrong, better or worse, it is just useful to know what type of team you are coaching. Each has their own unique set of needs and require a different approach to applying the Edge Dynamics.

As with many things in life, when it comes to a team, size does matter. The optimal size of a team will depend on whether it is simple or complex. Simple teams can be much larger and still be effective. Complex teams need to be much smaller – but not too small – to enable team members to effectively manage all of the Relationships they need. Here, collaboration is key, but it takes time and if too many people are involved, you risk over-collaboration and inefficiency.

CHAPTER 8

Creating a team Reason

The team need to get really clear about their purpose and value to the organization as well as individual team members' connections to that reason. This is the team's Reason for being and the starting point for everything.

What is Reason?

Reason is the team's *why*. It's their North Star, which provides direction to the team when they need it most. It's the reason *why* the team was created in the first place and a sense of the value the team brings to the organization and its customers. The organization will have created a design for the team and made some decisions about how the team is set up, its place in the organization and their expected outcomes and impact. They had a choice to set it up differently or to expect different outcomes. What is it that led to this particular mix of people, group of skills and knowledge? The team's Reason needs to be aspirational, values and principles based and most importantly be enduring and connect with everyone in the team in some way. This is about giving the team a single identity and a sense of purpose which connects them to each other.

When we talk to teams, they often mix up Reason and Results. They often think that *what* the team is expected to deliver (in other words their KPIs/objectives/goals) is the Reason they exist. But it's so much more than that. Results are important to a team, but to be truly motivated and fulfilled teams need a more compelling Reason than just achieving their objectives. A Reason lasts a lot longer than the team's KPIs.

The *why* is harder to create than the *what* because it is much deeper and more impactful for team members. Teams need to ask themselves a lot more questions to create it. Often assumptions are made, or the Reason is created in isolation from the team. The best team Reasons include the team in their creation and are not just created by the leader in isolation. Because the Reason is hard to create, it's often hugely valuable for you as team coach to support them in the process.

Why is Reason important?

There is a compelling business case for having a team Reason – in fact, according to McKinsey, 'there is a 1.9 times increased likelihood of having above-median financial performance when the top team is working together toward a common vision'.[37] If it works for a top team, it by extension must be important for any team to have a clear vision, a clear Reason for their existence.

People are more motivated when they have a strong *why*. That is why Reason is more than just a completion of a task or achieving a KPI. Team members need to understand the impact of the work that they are doing and that their work has meaning or contributes to the organization and its customers in some way. This contribution and meaning are what motivate people intrinsically. People also need to feel that the contribution they are making is bigger than just

---

[37] www.mckinsey.com/business-functions/people-and-organizational-performance/our-insights/high-performing-teams-a-timeless-leader-ship-topic

making money for some faceless shareholders. We used to hear a lot of organizations talk about adding shareholder value or value creation but that's not enough to motivate team members by itself. In any case, even shareholders themselves now want more ethical investments and are demanding to know that there is a sustainable approach to their return on investment.

We've already mentioned that the Reason is the team's North Star. The Reason helps them to make decisions on whether what they're doing will help them to achieve their *why*. It helps them to prioritize their Results and the things that really matter. Without a *why* there's danger a team's motivation will be left up to chance and the team may be missing an opportunity to really engage at a deeper level. Reason has always been important, but we notice it even more with new Generation Z employees entering the workforce, for whom '42% would rather be at a company with a sense of purpose, rather than one that pays more'.[38]

When we look at the neuroscience of motivation, we find that when you think about *what* you do at work your neocortex (in other words, your thinking brain) is triggered, it lights up – but this is not where motivation lies, just satisfaction. When we think about *why* we do something, our limbic system (in other words, our feeling brain) is triggered and lights up – this is where true motivation, passion, dedication and fulfilment lie. If we want someone to feel really motivated, we have to light up their limbic system. This comes from the *why*.

[38] www.forbes.com/sites/barnabylashbrooke/2022/08/24/its-time-to-retire-lazy-generalizations-about-gen-z-in-the-workplace/?sh=3f74d-5b5afe3

The impact of Reason on team performance

Having a compelling Reason results in a positive impact on the team's performance. Without it, team members can feel like the relentless Results focus is never-ending and without broader purpose. It can feel like their only reason for existence is to deliver short-term KPI-driven goals. And where's the fulfilment in that?

A compelling Reason connects team members to others in the team and creates a single entity with a shared common purpose. It also taps into team members' intrinsic motivations and gives them a sense of pride in the team's impact. This will get them out of bed in the morning and help them to enjoy their work every day.

We know, from research, that when people are motivated, they go the extra mile. They give discretionary effort and energy which means that their output is superior. This doesn't mean that they work longer hours (which let's face it is often unsustainable anyway) but they will definitely work smarter and collaborate more effectively with others. Working in this way re-energizes and refreshes the team and is ultimately much more rewarding for them. It also enables them to tap into their creativity and innovation more easily, as they take in a broader context.

When a team has a compelling team Reason, they are connected to each other in such a way that it creates a strong bond and sense of belonging. When this is in place, the team feels that they can achieve against the odds and capitalize on their unique sense of identity. This attracts others to the team – who doesn't want to part of something so rewarding?

The four levels of Reason

There are four levels of Reason: individual, team, organization and society. Let's look at each in turn:

1) Individual

Each of us has a Reason why we come to work each day – our own personal purpose. You might call this your values or your motives and it's very personal to each of us. People are like icebergs; 90% of an iceberg is under water. So, if people are like icebergs, 90% of us is hidden, not seen by others. The bit above the surface that people see of us is our behaviour – so how we do things on a day-to-day basis. And that behaviour might change in different contexts. Under the surface of the water, what people don't see of us are our motivations, our values and our beliefs. These things drive our behaviour. This is *why* we do things.

Our values are the things that we are often prepared to stand up and fight for. They can therefore be the source of conflict in a team if people don't respect other people's values.

It's amazing what a difference it can make in a team when people share and understand each other's values and it's easy to talk about them, as they just *are*. People are often surprised how rarely money appears in their values. If it is there, it's usually about what money means to them, like contribution or security or abundance, rather than just money itself. And that's because money can be a big demotivator if it's not present but is usually not a motivator in and of itself.

It's useful for the team to share their personal values with each other to maximize the chances of them being fulfilled, and to help them to notice the similarities and differences in each other's values. People might name their values differently (e.g. respect and integrity) and yet when you hear them describe what those values mean to them, you can see that there are some very similar themes. Similarity is important for bringing a team together and showing that they are connected to each other. In the same way, differences enrich the team and bring different perspectives and thinking to them. Problems can be solved more easily, in diverse ways.

When values are not fulfilled in a team or are compromised in some way, team members can be very disengaged and demotivated. At worst, they may even leave the team. You could coach a team to explore what would cause each team member to leave the team. In our experience of coaching lots of teams on their values, it's usually linked to one of their most important work values and many team members will describe times when they have left a team because that value has been unfulfilled. This exercise also develops vulnerability-based trust.

When conflict occurs in a team, invariably it is due to a value being 'stepped on' or challenged in some way. For example, a team member might accuse a colleague of treating them unfairly and if fairness is an important value for the colleague being accused, fireworks can follow! Understanding each other's values helps team members understand why a conflict has occurred and enables them to adjust their language, apologize if necessary and move forward from the conflict.

For step-by-step instructions on how to run a team values session, go to our website[39] and download the Values Exercise. This exercise is really safe to use with a team and create some quite profound disclosure from team members, opening up further opportunities later for growing vulnerability-based trust. It's also possible to use this exercise as a foundation for future coaching with the team. For example, you could run the values exercise with the team in one session, exploring similarities and differences and then in the next you could get team members together into pairs to discuss their values with each other and how they could collaborate more effectively with each other. Or you could present the organizational values and ask team members to

---

[39] www.management-dynamics.com/teamcoachingedge

notice the connection between their own personal values (or the themes across the whole team) and those of the organization. This creates a sense of place and belonging for the team within the organization.

2) Team

Team Reason is about understanding and getting really clear on *why* the team exists. Why is this team a team and not just a bunch of people who happen to work for the same boss?

What is the contribution they are aspiring to make together? What's bigger than just delivering a certain number of widgets or making a certain amount of money for the business? This is the team's *why* and is what will keep the team going even when the going gets tough.

Here are some examples of a few team Reasons:

- Delivering tomorrow, today (a transformation team)
- Deliver… together (a logistics team)
- Catalysing transformation and growth (a learning and development team)

We find that teams really love their Reason once they've got it as long it meets the criteria of Brief, Memorable and Inspirational (BMI). Brief enough that it is Memorable to team members and it just rolls off the tongue. Inspiring meaning that it connects with each person in some way and ticks off one or more of their values.

A team Reason is not for others and it's not a marketing exercise – it is just for the team, at least initially. It's about articulating something in such a way that it galvanizes the team towards a compelling purpose and unique identity. We'll talk a bit later about some ideas for how you could coach a team to create their Reason.

3) Organization

We then have the organizational Reason, the Reason the organization exists – again, this is more than just about making money or 'creating shareholder value' as it's sometimes known. Sometimes referred to as a mission, vision or purpose, Reasons are articulated by many organizations in different ways and the best ones, in our opinion, meet that BMI criteria as well.

Here are some examples:

- 'spread ideas' – TED Talks
- 'to accelerate the world's transition to sustainable energy' – Tesla
- 'to inspire and nurture the human spirit – one person, one cup, and one neighbourhood at a time' – Starbucks

The team Reason should align with the organizational Reason, if one exists.

4) Society

An organization doesn't exist in a vacuum and every organization has an impact, positive or negative, on society and on the world around it, of which it is a part. So societal impacts are important to pay attention to. There are so many things that different cultures value and place importance upon, and here are just a few that are part of the global consciousness right now, things like:

- Climate change – how are organizations impacting this? Are they behaving responsibly and making a difference, no matter how small? Or are they just ignoring or even exacerbating the problem?

- Connection – how do human beings connect with each other? Are they treating people well? Are they supporting connection between people?
- Inclusion – how inclusive a culture does the organization have? How inclusive are they with their customers?

Just a few thoughts, but these are the things an individual team member will be paying attention to, even subconsciously, and this will be impacting their own motivation and willingness to go the extra mile for the organization and the team.

Alignment of the Four Levels

These four levels are not isolated from each other – they are all interdependent and therefore need to be aligned to help the team realize the true potential of their team Reason.

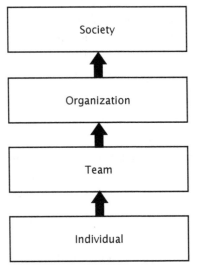

An individual in a team needs to feel personally engaged, understand what they need to be really motivated and know how that can be fulfilled by the team. The team needs to have a compelling Reason for its existence, which team members all need to be connected to in some way. This in turn needs to be linked to the organizational mission, which itself needs to impact society positively. This clearly describes the individual's place in the team within a wider system.

Coach team members to make that connection for themselves without leaving it up to chance. If the organization doesn't have a mission or minimal positive societal impact, that doesn't mean that the team shouldn't have a Reason – coach them to articulate it even without that explicit connection.

Creating a team Reason

So how do you go about coaching a team to create their Reason? Well, the first thing to say is that this is not necessarily a straightforward process and it depends a lot on the personalities of the team members involved as to whether they will find this easy or not. We would highly recommend that you help a team with this process. You can download instructions on how to do this from our website[40] – search for the Team Reason Creation Process.

We coached a team recently who had already spent six hours trying to create their team Reason. They got stuck, so called us in to help. We quickly realized they had been working on their *what*, not their *why*. So, of course, no one was getting particularly inspired by it. Once they shifted their focus to their *why*, it became so much easier. They had been trying to describe what the team does in an inspirational way and it's really hard to find inspiration in a list of day-to-day tasks. It's like us at Management Dynamics trying to find inspiration in *what* we do: 'we coach teams'. That's not particularly motivating or engaging, is it? It's *what* we do, but it's not going to ignite our team members' passion or excitement in any way. If we focus on our *why*, it all changes. Management Dynamics' *why* is: 'we catalyse world-class performance'. What a difference. This is inspirational and every team member can connect to it in some way, no matter what their role is.

---

[40] www.management-dynamics.com/teamcoachingedge

Then, we also set the scene by saying that the purpose needs to be BMI (Brief, Memorable and Inspiring). We will often start with a bottom-up approach – with what is important to individual team members. We kick off with the team members sharing their individual Reason/values with each other and then doing group work to brainstorm a team Reason together.

Another option is to start with what the team wants to be known for or how they want their customers/stakeholders to feel, then brainstorming the team Reason from there. Both of these approaches ensure that the team Reason is anchored in team members' motivations.

It can be an iterative process, with teams coming up with something, sitting with it for a few days/weeks and then refining it.

Sometimes a team will need to get into a creative mindset before doing this process. Think about how to set them up for success with this. We've used collages with magazines and pictures, postcards with images on them, getting out into nature, Lego®, anything which gets the team out of their normal day-to-day way of working and taps into their creative side.

Teams can also get stuck with this process – they can get tied up in knots about the semantics of a single word in a Reason statement. As a coach, it's important to know that this can happen and that it's normal. Hold onto the belief that just behind the stuckness is the outcome the team is looking for. Reassure the team that this is OK and part of the process. You might want to pause at this point and remind the team that:

- 80% is good enough
- They can refine it later
- It's only for them as a team

How Reason changes when the team changes

A team Reason can be quite enduring, but every now and then might need a refresh, especially if the team context or composition has changed significantly, such as a new leader starting in the team, a transformation, a significant number of new team members joining or leaving the team, etc. The key thing is to keep it alive and keep talking about it. Otherwise, it becomes another tick-box exercise with little meaning.

When new team members join, they need to be integrated into the team. This means inducting them to the team's Reason. A new team member joining doesn't mean that the team needs to assimilate them – they don't need to become like everybody else. However, it's an opportunity for the team to reassess their Reason and to realign everybody's motivations with the *why* of the team. We have seen a team create a word cloud of their values, which was very visual and a great tool for the team to use to remind themselves of their shared values. Whenever a team member leaves and a new person joins the team, they go through a process of sharing their values with the new team member, hearing that person's values too and creating an updated word cloud for the team values.

The links to other Edge Dynamics

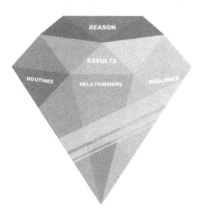

Reason is perhaps the most fundamental Edge Dynamic and holds all the others together. It is like the team's North Star and without it the team is directionless and solely task focused. When a team has a clear Reason, it has strong motivation, which will keep them going as a team when times are tough and ambiguous. It does this in a way that no other Edge Dynamic can. When a team's Reason is clear all the other Edge Dynamics become easier to establish and improve.

The connection to Results

Just like Reason, Results is about clarity. However, Results on their own are very functional, operational and, let's face it, possibly boring! The team's Reason brings life and purpose to its Results.

The connection to Relationships

Relationships are deepened by a team Reason. The Reason creates a shared purpose and sense of identity of the team as a single entity which connects team members to each other beyond just the task they are doing. It encourages collaboration for a purpose which is higher than just delivery of a KPI.

The connection to Routines

Routines can easily get out of date and by checking regularly how the team's Routines support their Reason, the team can ensure they are always fit for purpose.

The connection to Resilience

Resilience relies on a strong team Reason, as it provides motivation for the team to keep on going even when the going gets tough. It enables the team to bounce forward after setbacks as it focuses the team on their Reason even when 'failures' happen. When a team has a clear Reason they can more easily re-energize and self-motivate towards their purpose. They support each other more readily when energy is low and their shared purpose glues them together as a team.

> ### The case study team
> We introduced the case study team to you in Chapter 5, and discussed their context, their aspirations and Advantycs® diagnostic results. Here we will look at the team again in the context of Reason. Although they scored high on this Edge Dynamic overall, the team identified some areas for improvement, particularly around the team members' understanding of their own individual motivations and their connection to the team Reason. The team decided that they would like to work on their values. So we ran the Values[41] Exercise with the team, enabling them to articulate their own values and how that connected to their motivations in the team. It also helped them to understand each other's values and what makes them tick. This exercise was also great for catalysing a conversation about behaviours in the team. The team then spent some time creating their team Reason statement which was brief, memorable and inspirational. The team loved their team Reason, getting very excited about it and thinking about how they could bring it to life in their work and team meetings.

---

[41] See www.management-dynamics.com/teamcoachingedge

Creating a team Reason – a summary

Reason is the team's *why*. It provides direction to the team when they need it most. It's the reason why the team was created in the first place and a sense of the value the team brings to the organization and its customers.

People are motivated when they have a strong *why*. Team members need to understand the impact of the work that they are doing and that their work has meaning or contributes to the organization and its customers in some way.

A compelling Reason connects team members to others in the team with a shared common purpose.

There are four levels of Reason:

- Individual
- Team
- Organization
- Society

These four levels are all interdependent and therefore need to be aligned to help the team realize the true power of Reason.

Make sure that the team Reason is:

- Brief
- Memorable
- Inspiring

The team should keep their team Reason alive by talking about it regularly. It may need a refresh when significant changes impact the team.

CHAPTER 9

Delivering team Results

The team should get absolute clarity about what they are accountable for delivering, in a way that is easily memorable and visible for the whole team. They should align everyone's objectives and share that with each other. Encourage teamworking across shared deliverables.

What do we mean by Results?

When we talk to teams, initially they will tell us that Results is the Edge Dynamic they need to work on the least. Leaders frequently score Results higher than their team members do on our diagnostic. This is because there is often a strong focus in organizations on KPIs/objectives, goals/targets. There is also an assumption that because people know what to do in their job, they are clear on what Results are required at the team level. However, this strong focus on objectives and targets in organizations often results in teams having vast numbers of KPIs to achieve. This leads to a lack of clarity at the team level but also at the individual level around what this team is ultimately accountable for delivering. It also leads to an inability to prioritize well and to focus on the activities that will make the biggest difference to the organization as a whole. Consider the 80/20 rule[42] – what are the 20% of accountabilities that will add the 80% of value to the

---

[42] https://en.wikipedia.org/wiki/Pareto_principle

team and the organization? Less is more when it comes to team accountabilities.

We also find that there is a real lack of measurements of goals and objectives in organizations, particularly at the team level. Organizations are generally okay at making sure everybody has personal work objectives. They are often considerably lacking when it comes to making sure those individuals can measure their objectives and when we get to the team level, measurable team objectives are usually non-existent.

Clarity: The biggest gift a team can have

One of the biggest gifts that a team can have is clarity, and clarity on Results is essential for a high-performing team. Without it, team members are almost guaranteed to be working on their own tasks without involving others. We find that they might well be working at odds or cutting across the work of other team members. In fact, in the teams with the greatest lack of clarity around Results they're often competing and maybe even undermining the work of others in the team. This causes huge frustration, creates conflict and destroys Relationships in teams. So, you can see how essential clarity of Results is in a team.

A lack of clarity is a key root cause of overload and overwhelm in a team. Overload eventually leads to demotivation and ineffective work practices, which then leads to burnout and people leaving the team. Overload occurs in teams because people don't know how to prioritize or pushback on unnecessary requests. When they have clarity on the key things that the team is accountable for delivering, they are much better placed to be able to prioritize their work, push back on things that add less value and focus on the things that make the biggest difference to the organization.

Once a team has clarity of Results, it's important for them to keep reinforcing it, circling back to ensure that everyone is still clear despite new information. It's also important for them to refresh their Results regularly as the organizational strategy shifts or the expectations of the team changes.

Coach the team to create Routines (see Chapter 10) around how they measure and report on their Results as a team. How will they keep focus on their Results? How will they know it's time to adjust them? How do they bring new people on board to their Results? How do they adjust the team's workloads in times of absence or a lack of resource?

Alignment of Results

Just like with Reason, Results has different aspects which the team needs to pay attention to. Team members, of course, need individual objectives and KPIs and these are usually expected within an organization. Performance management processes usually measure and reward individual achievement of objectives. However, if they are going to harness the power of the team, these objectives should link into the team objectives and in turn the team objectives should connect into the organizational strategy.

Organizational Strategy

Individual Objectives

Team Objectives

Once a team has this true line of sight it should be easy for people to see where the organizational Results have been broken down into *what* the team is going to deliver and then where they as individual team members fit into that. Without this alignment, individual team members can feel like the work that they are doing is isolated and not making a difference to the mission of the team and organization.

In our experience, most teams are working on the right things, and they are working hard. They just fall into the trap of working on too much and diluting their focus or working on too many things that don't add the most value to the organization. They struggle to see the wood for the trees – to see the bigger picture beyond the task itself. They also struggle to prioritize what is the most important task to free up their time and focus for the things that will make the biggest difference. This means that they feel overwhelmed, under-resourced and under-appreciated. It's hard for them to pace themselves and plan how best to pursue their goals. Coaching a team to create clarity of accountabilities and then to align them at all levels makes a huge difference to a team in terms of creating focus on the things that really matter and enabling a broader perspective.

Taking a systemic view, where the team looks at all the elements which they impact and which impact them, empowers the team to take a proactive look at what changes could occur and how they will respond. It also helps them to see where they can take action for greater influence in the wider system in which they operate. The team can create a map of the system using many different possible tools like Post-its, Lego, other objects, etc. This can enable a team to feel accountable and in control of what they do.

Collaboration

When you don't have clarity of Results in a team, team members invariably end up working on their own tasks in a siloed manner. One of the things that leaders complain about to us the most is a lack of collaboration in their teams. Usually, the root cause of this is unclear Results. It's not that team members don't want to collaborate with others, they just don't know enough to do so well. Most team members just don't have enough clarity to collaborate with each other. They're not truly clear on what everybody else is doing, how that links to their work and the value that they could add to other people and vice versa. In some cases, this can lead to duplication of effort rather than collaboration, where team members are working on the same task without realizing it.

Another benefit of clarity of Results is that it creates connections between team members. Just knowing what others in the team are working on creates a sense of solidarity, that they are all working together towards the Reason even when the work itself is quite separate. It also offers an opportunity for people to support each other by offering ideas, best practices, suggestions and connections to other people outside of the team. It breaks down the sense of isolation that people can feel when they are working on a task on their own, which is particularly important in remote and hybrid teams. It also creates more opportunities for inclusion and an appreciation of the skills and contributions of others in the team. This then creates more opportunities for real collaboration in the team.

Over-collaboration

Some teams complain bitterly about a lack of time when we suggest that they should collaborate more effectively with each other. When this happens, it's often a signal that the team is 'over-collaborating'. What do we mean by this? This is when team members find themselves frequently in back-to-back meetings with each other all day long, with no pause for breath, or when they are reluctant to attend team meetings or find themselves doing other things while at team meetings because they are not getting the value they need from those meetings. And it's not just meetings, it's other forms of collaboration too – instant messaging, email, text messages, phone calls, in fact any way in which team members communicate with each other. If these things are not well managed by the team's Routines, the team will be in danger of over-collaborating and this will impact the Results of the team. In a team which is over-collaborating, things often get over-complicated, progress is slow and the team can repeatedly make poor decisions.

The organizational culture can impact the feeling of over-collaboration – what are the general expectations within the organization? Do people expect to be involved, included and consulted in everything? Do team members find they need a meeting to plan a meeting and those meetings involve casts of thousands? Can team members easily manage these expectations or does going against that culture feel like pushing water uphill? In some cultures, it can feel like it goes against the grain to be really discerning about who needs to be involved in a task and who should really collaborate.

Over-collaboration can also be a sign of a lack of clarity and alignment in a team. Coach the team to check back on their Results – are people clear about the team accountabilities and how their individual accountabilities align with them? Can they see where the most valuable opportunities are for collaboration and where there is really no need?

The 'Big Whats'

It's all very well saying that you need to coach a team to create greater clarity but how do you go about doing this? We have created a simple and effective way to coach a team to get clarity on their Results that has been used effectively with hundreds of teams. It's an interactive, collaborative process that enables the team to understand all the tasks that they are doing and then group them together into what we call the 'Big Whats'. This process articulates the team accountabilities in a simple, easy to remember way. This also means that every team member can see where their individual accountabilities sit within the 'Big Whats'. They can also see what everyone else is working on, their connection to the 'Big Whats' and the opportunities for collaboration in the team.

We coach teams to articulate their 'Big Whats' and their connection to the Reason on one page in the form of what we call a 'Diamond Team Charter'.[43] The principle of having a way of visually representing the Reason and the Results for your team on one page is a powerful tool to bring this to life.

The 'Big Whats' Process

Here is a quick overview of the process:

Make sure the team have no more than five 'Big Whats' – they can have less, but not more.

1. Brainstorm accountabilities
   Get each team member to write down on sticky notes everything they are individually accountable for, one sticky note per item. Tell them to keep going until they have everything.

2. Cluster accountabilities
   Get the team to group the sticky notes together by theme – which ones naturally sit together? Get the team to put them into no more than five groups.

---

[43] For more information, see www.management-dynamics.com/team coachingedge

3. Write an objective for each group
    Each group should have at least one objective or
    KPI associated with it. For example, a 'Big What' of
    'business growth' could have an objective of 'revenue
    growth of 30% by the end of the year'.

4. Name the groups
    Get the team to name each group in such a way that
    it makes sense to others. Make sure they are Brief,
    Memorable and Inspirational (BMI).

5. Coach the team to make the 'Big Whats' visible
    Coach the team and find a way to make them (and
    progress against them) visible to everyone every day.
    For example, they could create a poster, put them on
    a whiteboard in the office, print them out and lami-
    nate them for everyone, put them on a team intranet
    site, etc. Whatever works for the team to keep them
    in line of sight.

Naming 'Big Whats'

It's essential for the team to give 'Big Whats' BMI names. This
is what helps the team to remember them, which is the key to
them using them in their work. The purpose of this process
is to give clarity about what they are working on and to help
them prioritize and identify areas to collaborate. The team
should remove any jargon, make them easy to understand,
make sure that they resonate and recall what the essence
of the accountability is to the team. The team may wish to
share their 'Big Whats' with people outside of the team – if
they don't understand straight away, the name is not right
yet. They may need to keep coming back to this over time to
refine it and find names that work.

What if?

What happens if not everyone's accountabilities map to the team's 'Big Whats'? This occasionally happens in a team and it might highlight an issue with the team's organizational design. If one person's accountabilities are at complete odds with the rest of the team the leader might need to ask themselves the hard question of 'does this role actually belong in my team?' The answer might be that it doesn't but they don't belong anywhere else either. Then they need to ask themselves how they can find some synergies between what they do and the rest of the team somewhere and somehow. Otherwise, that person will feel excluded from the team and they will lose any potential benefits of what they can bring to the team and vice versa. As a coach, don't let the team off the hook – coach the team to be inclusive and value differences.

Reviewing 'Big Whats'

We often get asked how often a team should refresh and review their 'Big Whats'. There is no hard and fast rule for this and it's not necessarily something that has to be done every year as the leader would with their team members' individual objectives. The 'Big Whats' are generally more enduring than a 12-month process. They are quite fundamental to the team and therefore, if you've got those 'Big Whats' right, the team will find that they last a long time. Having said that, it's good practice to have a routine for reviewing them every now and again. The team should review the team's progress against the 'Big Whats', the various activities and tasks within them and where the collaboration lies. The real value comes from the team regularly reviewing how they are doing, what they could change, what the priorities are and how they are going to achieve those 'Big Whats'. Something that might trigger a review of the team's 'Big Whats' might be changes in the team or in the organization. For example, if a restructure occurs and the expectations of the team have changed, usually this means that the 'Big Whats' need an update.

Aligning team members' accountabilities

Once the team have identified their 'Big Whats' the process doesn't end here. The next step is for team members to align their accountabilities more tightly with the relevant 'Big Whats'. The team should identify who is contributing to which 'Big What'. It's important that each team member contributes to at least one of the 'Big Whats', otherwise there may be an issue. Equally, the team should not expect everyone to be contributing to every 'Big What' in a significant way. This can just lead to over-collaboration, where everybody is involved in everything and this can lead to confusion and overload. Doing an alignment exercise is a great opportunity for individuals to look at the 'Big Whats' and reconsider their task list, removing any duplication or low value and redundant tasks.

Once the team have created alignment of accountabilities, the next stage is to encourage collaboration on the things that matter the most. They should not be looking for collaboration for collaboration's sake – this just creates more work for everybody and feels like collaboration is being done without a purpose. What they are looking for is collaboration with meaning. If the team use the 'Big Whats' as the basis for collaboration efforts, then people are collaborating with a purpose and on the right things – the things that really matter to the team.

Links to other Edge Dynamics

Results are crucial in a high-performing team and create clarity for the team on what they are accountable for delivering. They also create the foundation for success in all the other Edge Dynamics.

The connection to Reason

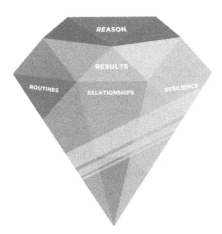 When we were discussing Reason in Chapter 8, we talked about how teams can get confused between Reason and Results (the *why* and the *what*). It's essential when talking about Results that they are connected to the Reason. *What* the team is accountable for doing has to be based on *why* they're doing it in the first place. Being able to articulate how the team's Results support the pursuit of the team Reason is essential for any team.

When a team works on tasks in isolation of the Reason, they risk the work feeling relentless and without purpose. Remember, it's the *why* that taps into the team's intrinsic motivation which lights up how they feel about the work that they are doing. People leave jobs because they have lost sight of the Reason in that role and have decided to seek fulfilment of purpose elsewhere. The *what* is just not enough on its own.

The connection to Routines

Clarity of Results is crucial in enabling a team to design their team's Routines well. When they have clear, aligned team accountabilities they can be sure that the right Routines will be easy to identify and implement.

When a team has created clear team accountabilities, the team has a desire to have visibility of their Results, to track progress and keep the team on track. This is enabled by the team's Routines and helps them to not only focus on the value-added stuff, but also see the bigger picture.

The connection to Relationships

When a team has clear and aligned Results they create space for better Relationships in the team. When they have clarity and alignment, it is possible for team members to collaborate well because they have a visible reason for doing so. They are more likely to communicate well with others because they have a shared common goal. They are also likely to build trust with others because they want to prove themselves to be reliable at delivering what they say they are going to deliver. They know what people are working on and have a shared accountability, so they want to support their colleagues and vice versa.

The connection to Resilience

When a team is not clear on its Results, it's difficult to have high levels of Resilience (see Chapter 12). Clarity is essential to managing team members' workloads and without it they will likely feel overwhelmed and exhausted. When you coach a team to clarify accountabilities in the team they are getting two gifts at once:

- The gift of focus – focus on what adds the greatest value to the organization.
- The gift of seeing the big picture, line of sight to the organizational goals and the team Reason.

These two gifts at first glance might seem like they are contradictory – can a team focus while also seeing the bigger picture? We would argue that a high-performing team needs to be able to do both at the same time and that both are crucial to the Resilience of the team. We would also argue that it's impossible to do either without clear and aligned Results. When we have worked with teams on their Results, we have seen very clear improvements in the teams' Resilience.

A high-performing team consistently achieves its KPIs, regardless of the challenges that pop up. They have the Resilience to keep going, even when the going gets tough. They can reprioritize their Results as needed and maintain focus on the things that are absolutely essential to the success of the team.

The case study team

We introduced the case study team to you in Chapter 5, and discussed their context, their aspirations and Advantycs® diagnostic results. Here we will look at the team again in the context of Results. When the team dug into this Edge Dynamic, it became clear that they had a good understanding of their individual objectives and each other's roles and responsibilities at an individual level. However, they were not clear at all about what the team's objectives were, nor how to measure the team's Results. This illustrated beautifully their siloed mentality as a team. The team spent some time creating their team 'Big Whats', of which there were four. They defined measures for each of the 'Big Whats' and they did an individual alignment exercise to articulate how their individual objectives fed into the 'Big Whats'.[44]

---

[44] See www.management-dynamics.com/teamcoachingedge

Delivering team Results – a summary

Results are *what* the team is accountable for delivering. They are measured through team KPIs/goals/objectives.

One of the biggest gifts a team can have is clarity, and clarity of Results is essential for a high-performing team. Teams with the greatest lack of clarity around Results are often competing and maybe even undermining the work of others in the team. A lack of clarity is a key root cause of overload and overwhelm in a team.

Team Results are multi-layered and there needs to be alignment at all levels: individual objectives should link into the team objectives and in turn the team objectives should connect into the organizational strategy.

Clarity of Results creates connections between team members and enables collaboration in the team which enables opportunities for team members to offer each other ideas, best practice and suggestions. This is also the foundation for complex problem-solving.

Over-collaboration can also be a sign of a lack of clarity and alignment in a team. Coach the team to check back on their Results – are people clear about the team accountabilities and how their individual accountabilities align with them?

Use the 'Big Whats' Process to coach the team to create clarity of the team's accountabilities in a simple, easy to remember format.

Results impact all the other Edge Dynamics positively and pave the way for a high-performing team.

CHAPTER 10

Building team Routines

The team should ensure all their Routines (meetings, ways of working, etc.) drive all the other Edge Dynamics and support high performance rather than interfering with it. They should know how to make decisions.

Defining Routines

Routines are a team's ways of working. The rhythms, tools and processes they use to get things done. This includes how they keep each other informed and up to date on the various tasks, projects and information they need to deliver their Results well. It's also about how they make decisions and who needs to be involved. It includes reviews of workloads and changes that are coming up which might impact the team and where adjustments might need to be made. Routines enable the Edge Dynamics in the team to work smoothly. They need to be designed well.

Routines dictate the pace of a team and if they're not careful, can get in the way of the effectiveness of the team and slow it down. Routines can sometimes be heavy, burdensome, administrative or even bureaucratic and out of date. Routines should allow the team to work at a pace that really suits them and the work that they are doing. At their worst, Routines will destroy Relationships (Chapter 11), undermine their Results (Chapter 9), obscure their Reason (Chapter 8) and destroy the team's Resilience (Chapter 12). They may contribute to burnout and absence in the team so coach the team to make sure that they design them well. How often does the team hear people saying: 'Oh no, not another meeting!' or 'that meeting was a waste of time' or 'I have to complete another spreadsheet for some reason, and I don't see how it adds value'. These comments are symptoms of ineffective or poor Routines.

Routines, like much in a team, need to be dynamic and ever-changing. Coach the team to constantly review their Routines ensuring that they remain fit for purpose and that they are driving all the other Edge Dynamics. Across the hundreds of teams that we have worked with, we see out-of-date Routines. This is often because a team has inherited old Routines or have just got complacent about how things are done 'around here'. Routines can easily get stuck or become obsolete when a team has not reviewed their Routines for effectiveness. In the first diagnostic, Routines are often the thing that is mentioned the most in the stop/start/continue comments from the team and they are almost always easy quick wins to change.

The team should look out for the signs that their Routines no longer work. For example, has attendance at team meetings dropped? Are people no longer following a process in the team? Are people using different methods to communicate with each other than they'd previously agreed? Teams can immediately change and adjust their Routines and the benefits are quickly felt. Coach the team to reflect on how they are continuously improving their routines and adapting them to the changing needs of the team.

Diagnosing the team's Routines

There are many Routines a team needs to consider. To help the team to reflect and prioritize where to start, we have created a Routines Diagnostic.[45] Simple and easy to use, it gets team members to rate 10 types of Routines that a team typically has on a scale of 1–5. Once the team have completed it and shared the collated results, coach the team to notice the themes and insights from the exercise, before getting them to prioritize and brainstorm actions. Routines are often easy quick wins and the team can think about how they can experiment with their Routines by trying something out and then reviewing how it works before amending it again if needed.

Creating a team rhythm

When a team is crafting their Routines, they should start by thinking about what rhythm they need to deliver on their Results, develop and maintain good Relationships and ensure high levels of Resilience. The team's rhythm needs to work with the team, not against them. What is the right cadence of meetings, communications and interaction that reinforces good Relationships and enables the delivery of Results? What cadence connects the team to their team Reason? What will enable a good balance of meetings versus time to actually do the work without creating overwhelm and over-collaboration? It's important for the team to consider when to discuss operational aspects. However, it's also important to coach the team to discuss how they are making progress against their Reason, what Relationships are like in the team and whether there are more opportunities for collaboration. They should consider how they can have more discussion and greater levels of

---

[45] Download this from our website at www.management-dynamics.com/teamcoachingedge

challenge in the team. Coach them to have conversations about development, both individually but also as a team.

Crafting team Routines is an art, not a science. It needs to be ever-changing to meet the dynamic needs of the team. Personality will play a big part in how they craft the rhythm of their team Routines. For example, the introverts in the team will need time to reflect and prepare for meetings and may find spending all their time in meetings frustrating and demotivating to the point of burnout. Likewise, the extraverts will need time to discuss and think out loud to come up with new ideas and move their work forward. Striking a balance for both needs is essential. They will also need to consider the experience levels within the team. Less experienced people might need more contact time and more support in terms of connecting with others. This enables them to learn, bounce ideas off more experienced people and build their confidence. Others might be more able to steam ahead without those interactions. Considering how they can develop more experienced team members as mentors for others in the team can strengthen Relationships.

It's very easy for a team to over-engineer their Routines. Less is definitely more. Coach them to build sustainable practices for reviewing their Routines – for example, to see how they can remove meetings, not add new ones in. They should continuously review how the team communicates with each other to make it simpler and easier for them. They should regularly look at processes to see how they can be streamlined or removed. The team should consider the tools used for all of this. Are they fit for purpose still? Are there other tools out there that would make things easier for the team? Could the way that the team uses tools be adjusted so that they become more flexible and more fit for purpose?

Meetings

Teams that we work with consistently complain about meetings and research shows that the number of meetings people spend their time in has increased dramatically over the last few years. According to the 2021 Productivity Trends Report, professionals are attending nearly 26 meetings a week, which equates to just over five meetings per day. That number has increased by a staggering 70% since February 2020.[46] Working virtually has created more meetings. The average meeting time was found to be 50 minutes and this means that people are spending over half of their week just in meetings. No wonder teams complain about overload!

When coaching a team to create their rhythm for team meetings, challenge them to consider who needs to attend. What is the desired outcome of this meeting for the team? What does the agenda need to be for maximum effectiveness? How will the team communicate that agenda so that the introverts have time to reflect and prepare for the meeting? How will they structure the agenda so that the extraverts have the chance to think out loud and brainstorm ideas? How will they ensure the actions are taken and that progress is made because of the meeting? How does the meeting add value to the whole team, not just key individuals within it? Does inviting everybody to the meeting create inclusion or does it just result in frustration for some who might feel they are wasting their time? Challenge the team's thinking about whether this meeting is needed in the first place. Is there another way to achieve the outcome? There are effective, interactive online tools where teams can share ideas without everyone being in the same place at the same time, such as interactive whiteboards and brainstorming tools.

---

[46] Reclaimai Productivity Trends Report (2021): https://reclaim.ai/blog/productivity-report-one-on-one-meetings

When considering who should participate in a meeting coach the team to think about who will be able to contribute to the outcome. This might mean setting up smaller groups for certain key meetings. It's important to be able to articulate to the rest of the team why they're not included in those meetings and for them to not feel excluded. The team should understand it's much more about effective use of time. It's also important for the team to know when to include everyone in these smaller groups to improve outcomes through brainstorming, challenge and playing the devil's advocate. This can strengthen connection to the team Reason and Relationships.

Decision-making: Who makes decisions in the team?

A key Routine in any team is how they make decisions. The team has to be clear on their process for making decisions and this must include who actually makes the decision. Is it the leader or are the team empowered to make some decisions for themselves? If they are not clear about this, either all the decisions will be made by the leader, or the team will make inappropriate decisions at the wrong level. If the leader is making all the decisions themselves, there is a danger they will become a bottleneck for the team and they will be waiting for the leader's decision before they can progress on things. This can slow work down. From research, we know that a team makes better decisions than one person alone.[47] This is because teams will debate and brainstorm options more effectively than one person will on their own. It's also because many decisions require complex thinking, which is harder to do alone.

---

[47] www.forbes.com/sites/eriklarson/2017/09/21/new-research-diversity-inclusion-better-decision-making-at-work/?sh=68bcdc674cbf

If the leader is holding on to too many decisions them-selves, they might be unable to take a vacation without their team members getting in touch with them. They might find that their availability to make a decision dictates the speed at which that decision can be made. Coach the leader and the team to discuss whether the leader really needs to make that decision. This is important to ensure that decisions are being made at the right level. The team should consider the impact changing circumstances can have. It's appropriate for the team to say 'most of the time, when things are normal, the leader doesn't need to be involved. However, if the situation changes or there's a crisis the leader needs to be informed or involved.' Often leaders hold onto decision-making because of the fear of a potential crisis, regardless of whether there really is a crisis. This disempowers the team and places an over-reliance on the leader.

We talk about the processes that you can use for gaining agreement with decisions that are made in the team under Relationships (Chapter 11). We also discuss how to get commitment from the team to decisions once they have been made. It's also important to have a Routine for documenting the decisions that are made by the team, to keep track of those decisions and their associated actions. How will they document, record and track progress of decisions that they make? Some teams that we work with use a decision tracker spreadsheet which lists all of the decisions that they've made as a team and associated actions, along with who's account-able for making sure those actions are followed up on.

Communication

There are lots of ways in which teams communicate with each other. The most obvious one is email and many teams use instant messaging services, collaboration tools and virtual meeting software. Coach the team to consider all of their communication methods, the tools they use and to agree clear guidelines and behaviours for their use. These should be reviewed regularly as part of their sustainable practice.

Processes

Another example of a Routine teams will no doubt have in the team is processes. These are standardized ways in which things get done in the team. No matter what kind of team you are coaching, they will have a process of some kind for various things. These may or may not have been documented and they will vary in complexity from one team to another. However, it is important for the team to be aware of what they are. The more they can streamline and simplify their processes the better. Likewise, the more they can document key processes in the team the more likely they are to follow them consistently without having to start from scratch each time.

While they are reviewing and challenging processes, coach the team to consider their purpose. In some organizations we have seen individuals, teams and indeed the organization as a whole use the processes to avoid risk, individual accountability, innovation and restrict change and adaptation.

Escalations

Escalations are when things go wrong in a team and the team bring something to the leader's attention. They are also when a team member asks for help at a higher level. Escalations are important in a team and they can be a symptom of other things going on in the team at a deeper level. Coach the team to look back and notice what kinds of things are being escalated and what might be driving those escalations. There are four main reasons why team members escalate things:

1. Capability – they don't have the capability to complete the task
2. Confidence – they don't have confidence to solve the problem
3. Knowledge – they don't have enough knowledge to inform a decision or solve a problem
4. Authority – they do not perceive that they have the authority to make the decision or solve the problem

Once the team have identified the most frequent causes of escalations, they can take action to fill the gaps that they've identified.

Planning and adjusting work

Workload is the number one issue we hear about in every team. There is always more work than any team can ever complete. Learning to review, prioritize, reallocate and adjust work is a critical skill for teams. One of the benefits of a high-performing team is using the whole team as a pool of resource for work. The whole team should feel accountable for the team's Results and should regularly review how they are doing and where work needs to be adjusted. New work will come in and priorities might have to shift. What Routines do they need to have in place so that all team members are a part of this review process? How can they ensure that they feel that they can contribute by offering more resource to other team members?

Engaging externally (e.g. customers, suppliers, partners)

Teams don't operate in isolation. They are part of a system of customers, stakeholders and other teams inside and outside the organization. It's therefore important to consider how the team engages with each of these groups and how they manage relationships more effectively. To build strong relationships with all of these different parties, the team needs to think about what regular Routines are in place and what communications and information processes need to be established. The team should review what they currently have in place, then identify what works and what needs to be changed.

Accountability

In a good team, we see leaders effectively holding their team accountable for both the Results and Relationships in the team. In a high-performing team, we see team members taking on this role themselves. They hold each other mutually accountable for doing what they say they're going to do. What does this look like? In a good team if somebody doesn't deliver on something that they said they were going to, other team members may go to the leader and tell them. The expectation is that the leader will resolve it for them. In a high-performing team, team members will go directly to the person who has under-delivered and talk to them directly about it. They will do so in a manner of constructive challenge without it descending into destructive conflict. They will try to support and understand the other team member in what's preventing them from meeting their commitments. This is a fundamental difference between a good and a high-performing team – one which makes an enormous impact on the Results and Relationships in the team. Having Routines which enable accountability in the team is important.

The links to the other Edge Dynamics

Routines are key to how the team operates together. When the Routines are fit for purpose, it creates a foundation for the other Edge Dynamics to be optimally successful.

The connection to Reason

A high-performing team has a Routine for reviewing and refreshing their team Reason regularly. They also have a Routine for reconnecting with their team Reason, even if they don't change it. They regularly discuss the Reason and bring it into their everyday operation.

The connection to Results

A high-performing team recognizes that Results require regular focus, tracking and review. This means that Routines for Results are essential. Without them, a team never really knows where they are in relation to their Results. Are they performing or not? If they don't adjust their 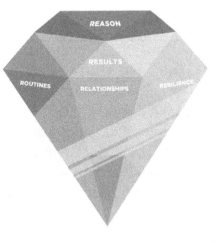 Routines, their Routines may no longer enable the delivery of Results and may in fact get in the way.

The connection to Relationships

Poor Routines can be very damaging to Relationships in a team. When Routines are ineffective, they can create frustration and conflict and undermine collaboration in a team. Effective Routines support the development of Relationships in a team by encouraging collaboration and communication amongst team members.

The connection to Resilience

Ineffective Routines can wear people down by wasting their time and sapping them of energy. Meetings are a great example of this – long meetings with a lack of focus and outcome truly frustrate people and exhaust them. The ineffective use of tools such as email can also create huge workloads which add little value and drain team members of energy. Effective Routines have the opposite effect and help people to manage their energy levels and workloads effectively while also providing the opportunity for people to support each other in the team.

The case study team

We introduced the case study team to you in Chapter 5, and discussed their context, their aspirations and Advantycs® diagnostic results. Here we will look at the team again in the context of Routines. We supported the team in reviewing their Routines and they identified their biggest frustration was their monthly team meeting. At six hours' duration online (meaning the team members in the USA and Singapore were working at unsociable hours), they found it boring, tiring and mostly irrelevant. Usually, it started with

---

every team member giving an update on their area of the business and this took up most of the meeting. If they did discuss something strategic, they often left the meeting unclear of the decisions that had been made and not having bought into those decisions which were clear. The team decided that they would redesign this meeting cadence. It was a relatively quick win (as Routines so often are) and became a two-hour strategy session with a focus on reviewing their 'Big Whats'. Once a quarter they would get together for a full day face to face, half of which would be strategic and the other half team development and social. They tightened up their decision-making process and assigned a decision tracker at each meeting who summarized the decisions that had been made in that meeting and checked in for clarity and buy in. They also agreed a process for having ad hoc meetings with smaller groups of team members and how they would keep the wider team informed.

Building team Routines – a summary

Routines are the team's ways of working and they interact with Relationships and Resilience to support *how* the team operates. Routines enable the Edge Dynamics in the team to work. They need to be designed well.

Routines, like much in the team, need to be dynamic and ever-changing. Coach the team to constantly review their Routines to ensure that they remain fit for purpose and that they are driving all the other Edge Dynamics. They need to be ever-changing to meet the dynamic needs of the team.

Use a Routines diagnostic to help the team to review their Routines, notice the themes, prioritize and take action. Encourage an experimentation mindset.

The team should design the team's Routines by first of all thinking about what rhythm they need to deliver on their Results, develop and maintain good Relationships and ensure high levels of Resilience.

The team should also design their team meeting cadence carefully and consider the frequency, attendees and agenda.

The team needs to be clear about who makes decisions on what. A team makes better decisions than one person alone so how can they ensure that the team members are involved appropriately in decisions and that the leader doesn't make all the decisions themself?

There are lots of ways in which teams communicate with each other. The most obvious one is email and many teams use instant messaging services, collaboration tools and virtual meeting software. Coach the team to consider all of their communication methods, the tools they use and to agree clear guidelines and behaviours for their use. These should be reviewed regularly as part of their sustainable practice.

In a high-performing team, team members hold each other mutually accountable for doing what they say they're going to do. The team should create accountability in the team.

CHAPTER 11

Deepening team Relationships

The team should build the appropriate levels of trust and ensure diverse opinions and points of view are embraced. They should disagree well and overcome conflict.

Definition of Relationships

Relationships are the cornerstone of a high-performing team and if a team wants to fulfil their potential, they need to invest in creating high quality relationships. Without effective Relationships, a team is not a team – they are just a bunch of people who all happen to work for the same leader. Relationships are, in essence, the interactions between the individuals in a team and how much value those interactions bring to the team and the achievement of their Results and Reason.

Having great Relationships doesn't mean to say team members have to be best friends with everybody in the team but what they do need is to have mutual respect, understanding of each other and a way to communicate and collaborate that's truly effective. The team needs to feel free to share their opinions and to have their opinions listened to.

The benefits of great Relationships

Relationships help the team make great quality decisions. Team members make better decisions when Relationships are good because it means they get challenge, discussion and ultimately greater buy in from their colleagues. Also, when teams have better Relationships, they have more fun and enjoyment in the work they are doing. Human beings are social animals, which means that they like to feel connected to others and enjoy the community that comes with a sense of team. If there's one Dynamic that at the end of the day really makes the difference to a high-performing team, it's the Relationships.

Relationships are the foundation of a high-performing team and investing in building them is essential if the team wants to get beyond mediocre to high performance. Most people resonate with this in some way at an intuitive level. However, Relationships will also be the downfall of a team as no team can remain high performing if Relationships aren't great. This is the key to sustaining high performance over a long period of time.

In the absence of all the other Edge Dynamics, good Relationships enable a team to deal with change, volatility and ambiguity for short periods of time. They are the glue that can hold a team together for a while. Teams are dynamic and so if the Relationships are good this means that the team has the flexibility to support each other as they shift their focus.

However, this will not sustain a team for very long and our experience shows that all the Edge Dynamics are essential for sustaining long-term high performance.

At the same time, without good Relationships, no matter how strong the team is, or all the other Edge Dynamics are, the team will start to get frustrated with each other and the sense of community will disintegrate. No team can withstand this for long.

The complexity of Relationships

Relationships are also the most complex of all the Edge Dynamics. Teams are made up of people, and people are complex beings. They are all different and have different needs. Relationships are also not static, they are always changing. People come and go within the team and every time a new person joins the team the team changes. Every time somebody leaves the team the team changes. This means that Relationships are incredibly dynamic and constantly need investment and effort to maintain them over time.

Teams are an organic system. The system consists of key players and interactions which are all interconnected. Many of those connections are explicit and we can see what they are, but many of them are implicit and are harder to identify. For example, you can explicitly see who gets on well within a team. They might meet each other for a virtual coffee, or a social night out or just choose to work together regularly. Implicitly, it might be harder to identify where there are sources of tension or what really motivates a particular individual in a team. Team dynamics are more complex than we can ever imagine and sometimes we can be surprised by certain things that happen in teams.

Teams don't work in isolation. They are part of a broader context. A broader system of the other teams in the organization, suppliers and customers, all of whom have impacts on the Relationships within the team. Coaching the team to consider that wider context and the key Relationships that they have, not only within the team but also external to the team, is crucial to the team getting to and sustaining high performance.

Where do you start with Relationships?

So where does the team start when developing their Relationships? We have identified several skills that teams need to develop to be truly high performing when it comes to their Relationships. They are divided into two levels – the foundation skills that team members need to have good, solid Relationships, and what we call the stretch skills that will take your team to the next level. The team won't achieve the stretch skills until they've developed the foundation skills.

Foundation Relationship skills	Stretch Relationship skills
Team members understand each other and have mutual respect	Team members have vulnerability-based trust
Team members are clear about expected behaviours in the team	Team members are willing to admit mistakes
Team members strive consistently to demonstrate expected behaviours in the team	Team members ask each other for help
Team members demonstrate reliability-based trust	Team members constructively challenge each other in the service of better outcomes
Team members commit to decisions made by the team	Team members proactively include others

Foundation skills

These are the skills that team members need to have good, solid Relationships. To describe each of the skills in more detail:

Team members understand each other and have mutual respect

To have a good foundation of Relationships in a team, team members need to know each other well enough to understand each other's personality traits, what motivates them and what drives their behaviour on a day-to-day basis. When team members don't understand each other very well this can lead to misunderstandings and assumptions being made about what is driving that person's behaviour. It's particularly important, when the team has a very diverse group of people, to understand that people have different ways of looking at the world, different values and different ways of thinking. The team investing in understanding each other better can really ease some of those misunderstandings. As a team coach, challenge people to think about the view they have of what can be 'right' and to see that there can be many ways and many approaches to things. Evoke their awareness of other perspectives.

There are several different personality tools out there, all with their strengths and limitations. Our advice would be to pick a tool that works for the team. Does it resonate with them and their context? Is it easy for them to remember and therefore use? Can it help them discuss how they communicate and behave with each other? Does it promote curiosity about how other people see the world? Does it challenge stereotypes rather than providing excuses for certain behaviours? Does it encourage people to start to flex how they behave with others who might have a different preference from them? Make sure that you are properly accredited to use the tool (see Chapter 4).

Mutual respect comes from knowing each other better. This is about team members understanding each other's strengths. It's knowing a bit more about who they are as a human being and what they stand for. It's about under-standing their personal values and what's important to them in work and life, their individual *why* (see Chapter 8). It's about knowing a bit about the experiences that they've gone through and some of the challenges and achievements that they have had. Encouraging team members to share and learn about all of this will enrich and create the foundation of good Relationships in the team. Also, when new people join it's important for the team to have some way of inducting them into this process and building relationships.

All of this creates a sense of curiosity about people in the team who may be different from other team members. Difference is an interesting thing when it comes to human beings. We actively push against difference and look for simi-larity in others – it's very natural and is an unconscious, deep-rooted safety mechanism. However, in a team, difference can be incredibly valuable. It helps us to think differently about things and to solve problems in innovative ways. It helps us to make better decisions based on a broader perspective. Through difference, we face complexity with more ease. Embracing difference and helping people to move past their own desire for sameness is essential in a high-performing team.

With all of this, a one-off 'team-building event' *will never be enough*. The team will need to invest more time and effort than this and find ways to incorporate it into their day-to-day interactions with each other, otherwise it will remain an intellectual exercise and not have the full impact.

Team members are clear about expected behaviours in the team

Another skill that is crucial for creating the foundation of good Relationships in a team is for team members to be clear about the behaviours that are expected of them. All team members have expectations of behaviours. The trouble is they might have different expectations from each other!

Very few teams put the effort into clearly articulating and agreeing between them what they would like those behaviours to be. Or they may not know how to talk about them. Behaviours generally evolve over time and may or may not be constructive and helpful for the Relationships in the team. It's important to invest time as a team in carefully crafting the behaviours that you would like to see demonstrated.

This is where you can come in as a team coach. You can run a session, coaching the team to brainstorm and prioritize what those behaviours should be. Once they have agreed them it's important for them to make sure those behaviours are documented somewhere and reviewed regularly to ensure that they are still effective and driving the Relationships that they would like to have in the team. A typical team only needs five to seven of these expected behaviours to make a difference. Less is more!

Team members strive consistently to demonstrate expected behaviours in the team

Once the team have agreed what the expected behaviours should be in the team, it's then important to ensure that they demonstrate and live up to those behaviours. Remind them that they are on a journey as a team towards their expected behaviours and sometimes people may lapse. They are human. In those situations, it is important for the leader and team to hold people accountable for their behaviours and to move back to expectations and commitments as quickly as possible. If they don't have that conversation, the norm will slip and others will follow. As a foundation skill, the leader will need to hold each individual team member accountable for demonstrating these behaviours at the same time as each individual team member holding each other accountable.

One of the resulting outcomes of people not demonstrating the expected behaviours in the team is what we call 'destructive conflict'. What is destructive conflict? It's when individuals in teams say one thing and do something else. When they undermine and challenge people in a way that is not in service of the positive intent of the team. It is about showing themselves to be better or superior to others or it's about having another agenda and trying to influence the team to do something which is not in service of the team's Reason or Results.

It's also about how team members receive challenge from others. Do team members respond defensively or with anger to comments that are made about their work? Do they feel insulted by others in the team, whether or not that insult was intended? Is there a sense of competition in the team? Do people feel they need to compete for best position or leader's favourite? All these behaviours are not helpful or conducive to good Relationships in a team and it's important to ensure that the team has a way of managing this kind of conflict when it occurs. Coach the team to notice when it happens and to hold individual team members accountable for the impact they have on other people in the team through their behaviours. It's also crucial that team members manage their own reactions to other people's behaviour in the team. This enables them to manage destructive conflict and turn the team culture into one where constructive conflict is possible.

We're not talking about having no conflict in the team. The absence of conflict can be just as destructive as conflict itself. If the team never disagrees with each other, never says a cross word, never gets a bit heated, then we would argue there may well be a problem in the team. A bigger problem than anyone might realize. A little bit of healthy conflict is a good thing in a team, they just need a strategy for dealing with it when it happens, so that team members can get back to an equilibrium in the team. Conflict is particularly important when teams are stuck. Generating a bit of conflict by team members sometimes being a bit provocative can be a positive strategy for shifting the team and getting them out of that comfort zone and thinking differently.

Teams often try to avoid the conversation of conflict, but we would suggest that it's healthy to talk about what should happen when conflict occurs in the team. Coach the team to agree what's acceptable and what's not. What happens if a line is crossed? How do team members come back from that? Do they need to apologize to each other? All these things are healthy for helping a team to manage conflict well and to continue their own personal development. They should include something on conflict in their agreed behaviours.

Team members demonstrate reliability–based trust

Trust is an essential part of good Relationships in a team. Trust has two distinct levels. The first one is reliability-based trust. This is when team members trust that other team members will do what they said they were going to do. The second is vulnerability-based trust, which is a stretch skill built upon the foundation of reliability-based trust. We will discuss this later in the context of stretch skills for Relationships.

When a team has reliability-based trust, team members can predict that their colleagues will deliver on their commitments. That they will deliver a piece of work on time. That they will be available when they need them to be. This is essential for the foundation of trust in a team. Without it, a team will not be able to rely on each other and so cannot work interdependently. Instead, they will constantly doubt that their colleagues will do what they say they are going to do. They will question whether other team members will deliver to deadline, give them the support that they need and be available when they need them most. They will question their colleagues' performance.

So how does a team create reliability-based trust? This links back to the expected behaviours. Coach the team to include how team members will deliver on their commitments to each other and how they will hold each other accountable for this. Coach team members to communicate about commitments with each other openly and to ask questions to explore potential misunderstandings about those commitments.

Team members commit to decisions made by the team

Often teams face challenges when it comes to decisions – perhaps with the process of making the decision in the first place, but most commonly with the commitment to the decision once it apparently has been made. A couple of signs for the team to look out for are that team members act as if the decision never happened. They carry on regardless. Or that team members gossip about the decision with others inside or outside of the team, suggesting they don't agree with the decision that was made.

There are two steps to decision-making: gaining agreement and then gaining commitment. Let's look at each of these in turn.

Gaining agreement

It's critical for a high-performing team to be clear on the process they have for gaining agreement for a decision. Often in meetings, teams work based on assumption – this means that if people don't speak up, they assume they agree with what is being said. This is a big mistake. Silence rarely means agreement. In fact, silence can mean many things instead:

- I disagree but don't have the chance/don't want to say so
- I still have questions
- I'm reflecting and considering the options
- I'd like to explore different perspectives
- I have concerns
- I'm not paying attention to what is being said
… and many more.

To gain agreement, the team must first have a process for making decisions. To be effective, this process must be clear who needs to be involved in the decision and what their contribution will be.

There may be different types of decision that need to be made in the team. Each will have a different strategy for gaining agreement. Here are a few examples:

A strategic decision

A team needs to make an important strategic decision that has wide-reaching implications across the team and their customers/stakeholders. This requires everyone in the team to input and provide all their different perspectives. They will need to pay attention to impacts they may not have considered yet. Ultimately the final decision will need to be made by the whole team.

Updating processes

A team wants to review and update their internal processes. One of the team members 'owns' this process. They need to seek input and understand the implications of changing the process on the relevant members of the wider team. They also need to identify who is impacted, to what extent and they need to consider how to involve them and gain their agreement to the change. This will not require the whole team to be involved in making the decision but the whole team may need to be informed once the decision has been made.

Workload issues
A member in the team has raised an issue about the workloads within their group. They would like to discuss this with the wider team to see how the workloads could be shared differently. This may not require the whole team to be involved in making the decision but it would be useful for them to have an awareness of what's going on in the wider team. Here it's about redistributing work across the whole team as the team member is appealing for support and flexibility. A team discussion about how workloads can be redistributed even temporarily can highlight where strengths, transferable skills and capacity might be available in the team. This can provide a development opportunity for members of the team. So, what started off as a challenge can become powerful and beneficial for the team.

Gaining commitment
Once a team has agreed on a decision, the team needs to commit to the decision fully. This means that they support the decision, even if they disagreed with the final decision

that was made by the team. In practice, commitment means that team members will defend a decision both inside and outside the team.

For team members to commit to decisions that the teams make, they need to be able to discuss and pick apart that decision before it is made. This means that everybody needs to be involved in some way in sharing their opinion and challenging ideas. Without this involvement, team members may have lingering resentments and doubts that are not verbalized and considered in the decision-making process. This requires good levels of reliability-based trust and understanding of each other's different personality types. Coach the team to raise their awareness of both of these things.

So often, we hear of teams who revisit decisions again and again and they feel incredibly frustrated as a result. They feel like they are going round and round discussing the same things repeatedly when actually the decision wasn't made properly in the first place. A lack of commitment is what causes that repetition of decision-making. Team members sometimes may also have not realized when a discussion on a decision has closed and that it's now time to commit to and execute on the decision that's being made. Sometimes team members believe that the decision is still open for debate. Having clarity that the decision has been made is essential. Teams need a process for doing this. This links to Routines (see Chapter 10).

When somebody disagrees with a decision (which, let's face it, happens!), once the decision has been made, the worst thing that can happen is that they undermine that decision outside of the team. This is a kind of 'I told you so', passive aggressive behaviour. If this happens, it's important that both the leader and the team hold the person accountable for their behaviour. Coach the team to have strategies for dealing with these situations, such as agreed behaviours.

Stretch skills

These are the skills that will truly take the team to the next level. They won't achieve the stretch skills until they've developed the foundation skills. To describe each skill in more detail:

Team members have vulnerability–based trust

A good team has reliability-based trust, which as we've established earlier, means that team members do what they say they're going to do. When it comes to a high-performing team, team members have vulnerability-based trust. This is when team members know each other well enough to be able to share what their weaknesses are, where they feel less confident and where they might need help. Team members know that other members of the team will support them if they don't have the skills or experience to complete some new task or if they just don't have all the answers.

For a team to develop vulnerability-based trust, they first need to have a foundation of reliability-based trust. Team members need to have mutual respect – this is essential to get to this deeper level of trust. It takes time and effort to create vulnerability-based trust and there are many things that they can do to short cut the process and help them get there quicker.

We often see teams which have individuals who have vulnerability-based trust with one or two other people in the team. The difference between a good and a high-performing team is that in the high-performing team everybody is included in that vulnerability-based trust, even when people are quite different.

Asking people to share a little bit more about who they are as people, as opposed to just focusing on the tasks that they do at work, helps build trust enormously. As with most things in Relationships, this requires continuous investment and it's important to place a renewed focus on it when new people join the team. How does the team ensure that new people feel included and valued straight away and enabled to share who they are with the rest of the team as quickly as possible? Vulnerability-based trust is all about accepting that people are not perfect and everyone has areas to develop. Coaching the team to create a learning environment and development-based culture can support the move towards vulnerability-based trust.

Some of the teams we have worked with have done team 360-degree feedback processes. Everyone completes a 360-degree assessment and gets their own feedback. We've then created a team process where the whole team shares their insights and development actions and asks other team members for help.

Giving feedback to each other is also a way to develop vulnerability-based trust as a team. It needs to be done well and we've had some wonderful experiences with teams where they've spent time preparing appreciative and constructive feedback to each other. By the end of it, everybody has grown and is in a much stronger place particularly as they realize how much they are appreciated by everybody and how much support they have. Make sure that you set up feedback sessions carefully. Consider where a team is in terms of their trust levels – generally reliability-based trust is not enough. Start with appreciative feedback, then add in constructive feedback when the team is ready.

Team members are willing to admit mistakes

When team members are not willing to admit their mistakes, they may cover up and hide things that have gone wrong. This means that they and their team can't learn from them. It also reduces the likelihood of them ever taking any risks. Team members will seek a safe way of doing things to minimize the likelihood of making mistakes. Mistakes may only be uncovered when things are going so wrong that they can't be hidden any more, or when the person has left and someone else takes over. This builds distrust in the team.

When the team have vulnerability-based trust, they will find that team members are able and willing to admit their mistakes. They will proactively share their mistake and what they have learned with the rest of the team. They will not fear that they will be punished, humiliated or that it will be held against them by the rest of the team. As a result, team members will be able to take more risks, willing to try new approaches, tools and ways of working. All of this is the foundation for innovation and creativity in the team.

Team members ask each other for help

When team members are not able to ask each other for help they may try to carry on regardless and this can be the source of intense personal frustration and overwhelm. It can lead to tasks being late or of poor quality. It can also lead to burnout and an inequality of workloads in the team.

In high-performing teams, vulnerability-based trust also results in team members being able to ask each other for help. When teams have vulnerability-based trust, people know that they won't be judged by their colleagues if they are struggling with a task or decision. They know that the door will be open for support, brainstorming ideas and sharing resources. When team members ask each other for help, they can also assist each other to grow and develop through sharing knowledge and skills.

Team members constructively challenge each other in the service of better outcomes

In a high-performing team, team members regularly respectfully challenge each other. This is not challenge for the sake of challenge, it is for the sake of creating better decisions and outputs together. This can take the form of constructive challenge – which is asking questions for better understanding. This is when team members deliberately ask questions of what is being presented to challenge thinking, to help people think about different perspectives and to be open to new possibilities. Team members often need permission from each other to do this. It also requires strong levels of trust to avoid team members on the receiving end of this feeling they are under attack and criticized. When coaching a team on this, ensure at the start that everybody understands there is a principle of positive intent and that this process is all about improving outcomes for the team.

This relies upon the foundation skills being present in the team as well as vulnerability-based trust. Without this level of trust the likelihood of team members getting defensive and feeling criticized is high.

Educate the team so that they understand the need for good questioning skills so that things don't get personal. For example, they should not ask 'Why are you doing this?' (this question can create a defensive response in others), they should ask something like: 'What impact will this idea have on our customers?' This expresses curiosity and exploration. Paying close attention to the words that are used is important in constructive challenge. Here are some core principles to share with the team:

Giving constructive challenge:

- Avoid the word 'but' – replace it with 'and' ('but' creates defensiveness as it suggests that you disagree with what has been said)

- When asking questions, start your question with a 'what' or a 'how' and avoid 'why' questions (these are open questions that are curious and invite a constructive response)
- Don't expect an immediate response or even agreement. If it is a powerful challenge, it will be thought-provoking which means they will need time to reflect on it
- Signal to the other person that you are about to challenge them constructively by saying something like 'Is it OK if I offer a different perspective?', 'I'd like to suggest a different point of view' or 'I'm going to challenge your thinking here'

Receiving constructive challenge

- Thank people when they constructively challenge you
- Acknowledge a constructive challenge even if you disagree with it. Say things like 'that's a good question', 'that's a powerful insight', 'I hadn't considered that', 'that's an interesting perspective'
- Don't feel like you must respond or agree immediately. If you need time to reflect on it, say so
- Notice your reaction to the challenge. If you feel yourself getting defensive, consider what is causing this. Remind yourself that the other person has positive intent for the outcome

Not only is it important for team members to pay attention to the words that they are using when they constructively challenge each other, it is also important that they pay close attention to their tone of voice and body language. The tone of voice should be calm, curious and warm. Body language should be open and relaxed. Change the tone and the meaning shifts. People put much more emphasis on the tone of voice and body language than the words themselves. Once you've shared this with them, coach the team to reflect on how they put what they've learned into practice in their day-to-day work.

Another way in which constructive challenge can be used in a high-performing team is by the use of the 'devil's advocate' role. This is when team members deliberately take on the role of somebody who sees things very differently from the rest of the team. They can then purposefully challenge from the opposite viewpoint from the team. Team members can find this skill difficult to start with and need practice. The team could get one team member to play this role at each team meeting and rotate the role around the team so that everyone gets a go eventually. Coach the team to reflect on what works and what doesn't and how they could play the role even better next time, perhaps by stepping into the shoes of a particularly critical stakeholder for the team.

Team members proactively include others

Inclusion is important in high-performing teams. Here we are talking about inclusion at its most fundamental level, where all people within the team feel included equally in the activities of the team. This means that they have consistent amounts of airtime in the team, so they get to share their opinions and achievements as much as anybody else in the team. In larger teams, this clearly becomes much harder as including everybody takes more time the more people there are in the team. It is important for the team to consider how they structure team meetings and set up their Routines to ensure that people feel included in key decisions, discussions and activities within the team. Done poorly, inclusive meetings are long, many of the topics are irrelevant to participants and at worst a waste of time.

Inclusion doesn't mean the team sharing everything with each other all the time, it is about being included in the key moments that matter. It's about being included where team members can add real value and feel that they have a contribution to make. Real inclusion is about inviting in the quieter members of the team to the discussion. It's about recognizing that reflective people need time to consider their thoughts before contributing. It's about ensuring that the extraverts in the team stay quiet every now and again and let others speak. It's about actively gathering everyone's point of view to make key decisions. It's about inviting someone to share an opinion even when they have little experience in the topic being discussed. It's about helping people who are less confident in their opinion still to have an opportunity to share some thoughts. Coach the team to reflect on how they make people feel included at key moments.

When team members are included in a team, they feel a sense of connection and belonging. They feel that their opinion matters and that they are contributing to the team and making a real difference to their stakeholders and customers. They will gain confidence to share their opinion even more when they are included. This creates a virtuous circle, where more inclusion means more sharing of opinions, which creates more inclusion and a growing sense of belonging. When people have a strong sense of belonging, it creates huge loyalty for a team.

So practically, how can the team create greater inclusion? Here are some suggestions:

Decision round

When a key decision needs to be discussed, the meeting chair should go round each team member and ask for their opinion on the matter. Ensure that some ground rules are set for this with the team. For example, they could include: only speak when it is your turn; no judgement of anyone's opinion; there's no such thing as a bad idea; if you want to refer to anyone's suggestion, present it as a 'build'; question only for clarification/understanding.

Another way of doing this is to get each person to write a thought about the decision on a sticky note and put it up on a board/wall. Then discuss the ideas.

To use this tool to finalize a decision, go round each person and ask whether they are 'for' or 'against' the proposed action. Each person should explain their position, with no judgement or argument from other team members.

Opinion seeker role

The team could have a role called the 'opinion seeker' which gets rotated around the team. This person's role is to keep an eye on the quieter people in the team and to invite them into the conversation every now and again. Introverts will often wait to be invited into a conversation and this role makes sure that their voices and opinions are heard. The kind of things this person might say/ask are: 'xxx, I notice you've been very quiet in this meeting – what do you think of xx?', or 'I'd love to hear xxx's view on this'.

Be sure to pause and allow silence, which invites their response.

When new people join the team, it's important for the team to include them as early as possible in activities and get them to share their expertise and transferable skills with the team. This is particularly important when people are working remotely and is a way of connecting them very quickly to others with whom they may not have the opportunity to build a relationship with otherwise.

Going the extra mile

When Relationships are poor in a team people become much more selfish and will focus mainly on their own tasks and objectives. They may not even notice when other people in the team are struggling. The last thing they are thinking about is helping others.

When Relationships are good in a team, people will go the extra mile for their team members. They will try harder, they will support each other more and they will be available to give advice to each other when it's needed. They notice when they can help and they want to offer their support. Their commitment to the team and the team's Reason is greater. This means that they will sacrifice their own personal goals and agenda for the good of the team. People get a huge sense of contribution and well-being when the conditions enable them to do this.

Avoid forced fun

Social activities are helpful in building relationships in a team. Spending time together outside of work is a powerful tool for breaking down barriers, building trust and getting to know each other at a fun, more fundamental level. However, it must be done well, in an inclusive way and must consider a whole range of factors which might impact the individuals in the team in different ways. We would suggest that forcing people to have fun does not build relationships and what is perceived as fun by one person in the team might not be shared by somebody else. For example, some people in the team may find a human table football game fun, but when one team member has mobility issues it is excluding for them.

The team should ensure that everyone is happy to take part in social activities and that the timing works for everyone.

Team members who have children may find evening/weekend events hard to attend. Asking people to stay out very late may impact the team member with a long commute. The key is for the team to ask people's opinions and to make social events optional. Those who don't attend will feel excluded even if it was their choice not to take part. The point is not for the team to stop all social events, it's about choosing events that can be inclusive of everyone in the team. Or it may be a mix of events that can include the whole team over time. Or maybe they need to do something during the working day? Coach the team to consider all these factors when creating social activities.

The links to other Edge Dynamics

Relationships are the glue that determine how it feels to be a part of this team, which is a crucial element of performance. Let's explore how Relationships link to the other Edge Dynamics:

The connection to Reason

When teams work on Relationships, they are getting closer to what their own individual Reason is and therefore what the team Reason might be (see Chapter 8). Often, when we work with teams, team members share their personal work values with the team and notice the similarities and differences between their personal values. Values are a crucial part of who we are and what motivates us at work. They are also a foundation of Relationships. When team members understand each other's values, it builds Relationships and helps them manage destructive conflict. Here the team are effectively killing two birds with one stone and working on both Reason and Relationships at the same time. Relationships in teams creates a sense of connection and belonging and when we look at people's values in teams, we often see those words popping up. Connection and belonging are important motivators for a lot of people. As are things like trust, honesty, integrity and making a difference.

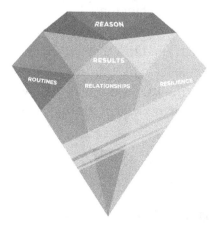

When teams look at their expected behaviours, they often see a direct connection back to the team Reason. By coaching the team on their expected behaviours, they are reinforcing and deepening the Reason why their team exists.

The connection to Results

When a team works on their Relationships they are providing the conditions for success in the team's Results (see Chapter 9). They are more able to work together well on shared team objectives. They are establishing the foundation for collaboration in the team and the sharing of ideas and best practice. This enables innovation, creativity and better problem-solving. The team is able to deal with complexity much more effectively as their Relationships give them the courage and the edge they need to face things head on.

People in the team are also enabled to deliver superior Results individually because they can share ideas, learn new skills from other members of the team and receive mentoring. This creates confidence at the individual level which means that they will be more likely to take risks and try new things. All these things together enable superior Results in the team.

The connection to Routines

When the team works on Relationships, very quickly any gaps in their Routines (see Chapter 10) will become obvious. They should identify the Routines that cause friction in the team either because they are perceived to be wasting people's time, because they are not inclusive of all team members or they are not in service of Results or Reason. Very quickly, the team will notice which Routines promote the behaviours that the team don't want to see. It will be important for them to adjust those Routines straight away to enable the behaviours that they want to see. Coach the team to reflect on how their Routines strengthen and enable Relationships and where they get in the way or at worst undermine them completely.

Beginnings and endings are important for Relationships in teams, so the team should make sure that they have Routines specifically around inducting new people to the team and people leaving. We discuss this in more detail in Chapter 12 when we discuss Resilience.

The connection to Resilience

When the team works on Relationships they are, by default, also working on Resilience (see Chapter 12). Resilience relies on strong Relationships. Humans are designed to be part of a community and at work the team is their community. The team needs good Relationships to have that sense of community support, so if the team wants to be more resilient, they should look at their Relationships. Coach them to reflect on where they are weak and where they need to be strengthened.

Isolation and exclusion in a team undermine team members' Resilience. Coach the team to reflect on how they create a sense of belonging, connection and inclusion as all of this is essential for Resilience. Relationships enable team members to share their mistakes, knowledge and skills. They also enable a supportive environment when mistakes are made that builds the ability to bounce back from setbacks.

The case study team

We introduced the case study team to you in Chapter 5, and discussed their context, their aspirations and Advantycs® diagnostic results. Here we will look at the team again in the context of Relationships. The team scored this Edge Dynamic moderately at 3.5 and in the discussions they realized that they have good levels of respect and reliability-based trust (with some way to go still) and very little vulnerability-based trust. This meant that people didn't share their opinions, particularly on other team members' areas of expertise. This was something that the team needed to edge towards, slowly but consistently over time. So, throughout the team coaching process we built in vulnerability-based trust exercises including Personal Success Stories and the Team Unknowns exercise.[48] We also coached the team to regularly review their Relationships.

Deepening team Relationships – a summary

Relationships interlink with the Edge Dynamics of Routines and Resilience to support *how* the team operates. Without effective Relationships, a team is not a team – it is just a bunch of people who all happen to work for the same leader. Relationships are, in essence,

---

[48] See www.management-dynamics.com/teamcoachingedge

the interactions between the individuals in a team and how much value those interactions bring to the team and the achievement of their Results and Reason.

We have identified several key skills that teams need to develop to be truly high performing when it comes to their Relationships. They are divided into two levels – the foundation skills that team members need to have good, solid Relationships, and what we call the stretch skills that will truly take the team to the next level. They won't achieve the stretch skills until they've developed the foundation skills.

Foundation skills:

- Team members understand each other and have mutual respect
- Team members are clear about expected behaviours in the team
- Team members strive consistently to demonstrate expected behaviours in the team
- Team members demonstrate reliability-based trust
- Team members commit to decisions made by the team

Stretch skills:

- Team members have vulnerability-based trust
- Team members are willing to admit mistakes
- Team members ask each other for help
- Team members constructively challenge each other in the service of better outcomes
- Team members proactively include others

When Relationships are good in a team, people will go the extra mile for their team members. Social activities are helpful in building Relationships in a team. Spending time together outside of work is a powerful tool for breaking down barriers, building trust and getting to know each other at a fun, more fundamental level. However, 'forced fun' should be avoided – the team should take care to include each other in defining what social activities take place and how to include everyone.

CHAPTER 12

Sustaining team Resilience

The team should continuously review their Edge Dynamics. They should regularly reflect on how to maintain their energy, motivation and endurance for high performance. They should look out for the signs that things need to be adjusted in the team, enabling them to flex and adjust to change.

What is team Resilience?

Resilience is a person's ability to bounce back from adversity. In a team context, the same definition applies, we just extend it a bit and change the emphasis from bouncing back to bouncing *forward* – the team support each other to come back from adversity even stronger than before.

A team is made up of a group of individuals and each person has their own level of Resilience by themselves. When team members collaborate with each other, meet with each other or interact in some way, team Resilience also becomes important. If people are excluded (or exclude themselves), don't collaborate and so on, then that will reduce the Resilience of both the individuals and the team. Low Resilience is infectious. People can unintentionally infect others with their state of mind.

One of the gaps in teams is that they don't often tap into the power of the team to create Resilience in the team. They just focus on their own individual Resilience. Resilience is also infectious in a positive way – the strength of one individual's Resilience can lift that of another team member. And the team also contributes to individual Resilience; teams provide many of the solutions to Resilience – connection, support, contribution, fulfilment of values and many more things which all build up our Resilience.

When people talk about Resilience, they usually consider it through one of two viewpoints: either individual Resilience or organizational Resilience. We would argue that team Resilience is also an essential viewpoint for creating high performance. Let's explore each of these in turn:

Individual Resilience

According to the American Psychological Association, 'resilience is the process and outcome of successfully adapting to difficult or challenging life experiences, especially through mental, emotional, and behavioural flexibility and adjustment to external and internal demands.'[49] When someone has individual Resilience, when challenges occur, instead of demonstrating unhealthy coping strategies (or just not coping), people are able to face difficulties head-on.

Organizational Resilience

Organizational Resilience is the ability of an organization to withstand crises, unexpected events and disruptions to their business by unforeseen circumstances. There are plenty of good examples such as pandemics, geopolitical tensions, financial market disruption and supply-chain issues. A resilient organization plans for the unexpected, actively

---

[49] www.apa.org/topics/resilience

manages its cash flow and reserves and adapts its business quickly to the changing environment. A resilient organization is constantly looking to the future to try and anticipate future challenges and plan their response.

Team Resilience

The critical link between individual and organizational Resilience is *team* Resilience. When a team has good Resilience they inject Resilience into the organization through anticipation of challenge and change in their area. They also assist individuals with their own personal Resilience by providing support, adjustment of workloads and ways of working. This is the key to sustaining high performance over time. If organizations want to truly be resilient, they need to focus on building team Resilience and yet it is so often overlooked. Many organizations have put in place excellent well-being programmes and support which is all about supporting individual Resilience. The impact of these efforts would be magnified if more of an emphasis was placed on the links into team Resilience.

If a team does not have strong Resilience, yet has high levels on all the other Edge Dynamics, there is no way they can be truly high performing. They will not sustain any performance levels they achieve for very long and a high-performing team gets to high performance and maintains it over time. This Edge Dynamic, more than any other, is the one that teams pay little attention to and yet it is the one that will enable the team to sustain high performance. This is the key to reaping all of the benefits of high engagement. In a resilient team, people feel satisfied in their jobs and deliver incredible results. Team Resilience is not just about managing what's right in front of you and being able to bounce forward from setbacks. It's also about being able to anticipate changes and challenges on the horizon and adjust their response. It's about preparing and being proactive for changes that are about to come along in the short, medium and long term.

For the team to be resilient, they need to plan how they are going to anticipate, shift and change to new requirements that come in. As new members join and people leave, they need to think about how they learn from their activities and projects and incorporate that learning into their future work. The team needs to grow and develop so that they are ready to take on new tasks, be innovative and creative and also to ensure the personal growth of each individual within the team. Coach them to reflect on all of this.

What do high-performing, resilient teams do?

It can be useful to educate teams that high-performing, resilient teams:

- Do more with what they have
- Work smarter not harder
- Take proper breaks
- Celebrate the small wins
- Laugh together
- Believe there is only winning and learning

Do more with what they have

High-performing teams are able to make the most of the resources that they have and stretch out beyond what they previously thought was possible to do even more. They don't necessarily need to ask for more resources. They challenge themselves to think outside the box instead.

Work smarter not harder

They work in smarter ways rather than harder through longer hours. High-performing teams look for ways to work more efficiently and effectively. This increases their capacity for greater things. They continuously review and remove Routines that no longer add value.

Take proper breaks

They understand how important it is to take regular, proper breaks that enable team members to recharge and recuperate. They encourage and assist team members to take breaks and ensure that they are true disconnects from the work without interruption. This includes breaks throughout the working day as well as vacation time.

Celebrate the small wins

They continuously celebrate the little milestones that added together make up big achievements. They know that this is key to sustaining motivation over long periods of time. They also celebrate individual successes as a reflection on the team.

Laugh together

High-performing teams have fun and enjoy working together, even when the work they do is high stakes. They laugh regularly and seek out moments of fun.

Believe there is only winning and learning

They don't believe in 'failure' as a concept – they see them as opportunities to learn and do even better next time. In this way there is only winning and learning.

Once they are aware of these factors, coach them to reflect on where the gaps are in the team and what actions they will take to build Resilience.

The impact of Resilience on sustaining high performance

When teams have low levels of Resilience, they can struggle to sustain high performance over a long period of time. Team members get exhausted, may burnout or lose interest in the work and seek other opportunities outside of the team. If they have high levels of turnover, lots of absence or sickness, we would argue the team probably has low levels of Resilience. Nearly every team scores lowest on Resilience the first time they run our diagnostic. Most teams pay little attention to Resilience, compared to the other Edge Dynamics. They may review workloads in the team and encourage team members to manage their own individual Resilience but this is usually as far as it goes and they don't harness the power of the team. Only the best teams pay really close attention to actively managing Resilience at the team level.

When teams have high levels of Resilience, they are capable of sustaining high performance over long periods of time. This means they can deliver at the highest levels, continuously.

The whole team is committed to supporting other team members to deliver superior outcomes. This means working together to manage the energy of the whole team, not just the individuals within it. The team sets a pace and adapts it so that they can sustain that level of high performance for everyone. When one person's energy levels are low in the team, the rest of the team adapts, supporting them to re-energize and adjusting workload to ensure Results are still delivered.

High-performing teams sustain high performance over time largely due to the fact that they are continuously learning. They pay close attention to what works and what doesn't and are curious about finding new ways to deliver Results. They're always asking the question 'how can that be done differently?' They use collaboration to simplify complex issues and to come up with innovative solutions together. The emphasis is always on 'us' as a team rather than 'me' as an individual. This means that the burden of Results is shared across the team. Individual team members benefit enormously from this as there are massive opportunities for personal growth, supported by the whole team.

The power of substitution

When we talk to teams, we often hear about the adrenaline and satisfaction that team members can get from a burst of energy around a particular deliverable. However, it's hard to maintain that level of output over a long period of time. People need rest and recuperation to have the energy that they need to deliver at that level again. This is where the power of team can really make a difference. When an individual tries to sustain prolonged periods of high output, they invariably can't do it for long. Physically, humans need a break. In a high-performing team, there is no need for a reduction in team performance because team members can substitute for each other. They can plan in breaks and rest time for physical, mental and emotional recharge. This means that the overall performance of the team is sustained and each individual gets time to recuperate and be ready to perform back at high levels again. In team sports, we see this happening all the time. Teams use substitutes to bring players on and off the pitch to compensate for a drop in energy levels from players who have been on the pitch for a while. Sometimes the team might also need a different skill for that stage of the game – for example when penalties are looking likely in soccer, teams may substitute their best penalty shooters onto the pitch.

Coach the team to think about how to bring this concept into their own context. They can this about how to substitute their key players when they need a break or specialist skills are required. Substitution requires good levels of collaboration, great Relationships (Chapter 11), efficient Routines (Chapter 10), excellent clarity of Reason (Chapter 8) and a laser-like focus on Results (Chapter 9). In fact, all the other Edge Dynamics contribute to enabling substitution to happen.

Flow

When a team has high levels of Resilience, the concept of flow[50] becomes possible more often in the team. A flow state, or 'being in the zone', is the mental state in which people feel fully immersed in what they are doing. They lose all concept of time, are fully focused, deeply concentrating on the work at hand and are really energized by it. Teams can get into a flow state too when they are collaborating, brainstorming and working on things together really well. High-performing teams regularly get into flow. People don't want to leave teams where this happens often.

Resilience by design

We know by working with hundreds of teams that Resilience doesn't happen by chance – it has to happen by design. There are many contributing factors to building a team's Resilience and it's a continuous process. In sport, teams train over time

---

[50] Mihály Csíkszentmihályi, *Flow* (2002).

to build up their endurance, their speed and their strength. They practise playing different positions in the team so that they can substitute for each other in times of injury or exhaustion. They develop deep expertise in specific skills which are required in the team and a team will never rely on just one person to have those skills. The team could reflect on how they can use this analogy within their team. How could they develop the team for Resilience? Resilience is not something that can be done 'to' a team, it's something they need to work on together. Team Resilience will also vary from team to team so it's important for the team to find their own strategies and ways of working that are effective for the personalities and needs of the people within the team.

Reduce potential points of failure to increase Resilience

Most teams have potential points of failure in the team and this will impede their ability to be resilient and maintain high performance. The team has critical tasks and skills which can only be done by one person in the team. When that person takes a vacation, is off sick or absent for any reason, that task doesn't get done, so productivity drops. This is OK if they can plan around periods of absence but sometimes absences happen unexpectedly or are long term.

Single points of failure can result in a team member feeling overloaded before they go on vacation as they try to prepare for their time off and overloaded when they come back as they try and clear the backlog that has built up in their absence, all of which causes their Resilience to drop. They may be tempted to check their emails regularly while they are away to keep that particular task ticking over, so that when they come back they don't have so much backlog to clear. This means that they are not truly getting the mental break they need from work to be refreshed and fully resilient on their return.

High-performing teams have no single points of failure in the team. They don't rely on one person to do a particular task all the time. They know what the critical tasks are and they invest in developing multiple people to do those tasks well. This includes some of the tasks which are carried out by the leader. A high-performing team can sustain performance without a leader for some time, although this doesn't mean they can do it forever. At a minimum, a team should be able to perform while people, including the leader, are on vacation. Coach the team to reflect on what their potential points of failure might be. Who currently has the skills to substitute and cover those potential points of failure if an individual was off sick or away for some reason? Who might benefit from developing those skills?

Create a culture of learning to increase Resilience

People often think of Resilience as bouncing *back* from setbacks. As we said earlier, we prefer to think of it as bouncing *forward*. This means they don't just revert back to how they used to do things, they learn from the experience and develop as a result. They are stronger in some way. In high-performing teams this also happens. When a setback occurs, the team bounces *forward*, having learned from experiences and challenged themselves to stretch, adapt and move to the edge. High-performing teams invite in challenge which creates the stretch, adaptation and learning without a setback needing to occur. They are then ready when setbacks do happen. There are a number of key things that high-performing teams should pay attention to when seeking to create a culture of experimentation and learning. This includes developing an agile mindset, experimentation, changing perspective and holding up the mirror. Let's look at each in turn.

Agile mindset

An agile mindset is one where all team members are open to looking at what they do as individuals as well as challenging how other team members are doing things. They look externally for new ways of operating – they are not afraid of trying to see the world in a different way and learn from all types of experiences and influences. It's a mindset of 'can do' and 'how can we do this differently or better?' It's a fundamental belief that anything is possible. As a team this is hugely empowering. An individual team member might lack confidence in one thing but as a team they know that everything is possible – the key is just to find the way.

Experimentation

Teams who have a regular practice of experimenting with how they do things are substantially more successful and resilient than teams who don't. Teams who experiment regularly are not interested in perfection first time. They accept that each time they have a go they're learning from that experience. It's more about the information that they gain as they experiment to build towards whatever the final output or outcome might be. All the big leaps in humankind, whether it's reaching the moon or developing a vaccine, have taken an experimentation approach. This is where people learn in small steps and build on what they understand each time. There is no fear or criticism of failure in this process. It's all about what information they are gaining to help them build on being more effective next time and having another go.

High-performing teams use an experimentation mindset approach in everything they do. They use it in how they deal with customers and practise different communication styles to see what will work. They use it in constantly challenging the tools that they use and how those tools could be improved. This doesn't mean that they go messing around with processes and ways of doing things all the time. They experiment in a controlled way with permission from the rest of the team. They have a routine for reflecting on what works and what doesn't; for planning experiments and managing the risks associated with that. They review the results of their experiments and then decide what to do next. Coach the team to reflect on how they could experiment more. What conditions will they need to put in place to make sure that happens?

Changing perspective

High-performing teams don't just have one way of looking at things. They regularly change their perspective to see things differently and to notice things that they might not have spotted otherwise. They create Routines which help them to change their perspective on their work. They talk to people outside of the team to get different viewpoints and they identify experiences which will create insights and connections. These experiences don't need to be directly related to the work of the team to be successful. In fact, the more different they are the better. The most important thing is to be able to explore the analogy that the experience creates and bring that back into the team as learnings. We often see teams having enjoyable team-building days or social activities, but they are usually isolated events with no link back to the team's day-to-day activities. They may be fun activities but the power of the perspective that could be generated is not harnessed and brought back into the overall team.

Analogies are incredibly powerful ways to change a team's perspective. Coach the team to consider what analogies they could use to think about how they could see their work from another perspective. When they are doing team-building activities, they should ensure that they always do a debrief of the insights people have created about the team as a result.

Holding up the mirror

While looking outside the team really helps them to get a wider perspective, the team also need to look inside regularly. We call this 'holding up the mirror'. This is about creating experiences that help the team to reflect on how the team is working and what could be improved. It's also about helping the team to see how well they're demonstrating their expected behaviours and where they could create further opportunities from all the difference and diversity within the team.

As team coaches, we often help teams to hold up the mirror. We do this by creating team challenges and by doing team observations. Any experience which is designed to help them notice the Edge Dynamics within the team is useful. Using our diagnostic tool is also a way of holding up the mirror. Feedback processes can be a very powerful way for both individual and team development, this means helping the team to give each other feedback on what works and what doesn't in their Relationships with each other. High-performing teams build in Routines to regularly hold the mirror up for themselves and we know when they have got to high performance because they no longer need us to help them with this.

Anticipating changes in the team increases Resilience

High-performing teams are not static, they are dynamic. Members of the team will leave at some point and move on to greater things and new members will join. This is unavoidable and essential for the renewal of the team. Every time someone leaves or joins, the team changes fundamentally – in fact, they become a new team. When a team changes like this, Resilience can drop as the Edge Dynamics in the team are impacted. New team members require more support, don't have the same level of clarity as existing team members, don't have the same depth of Relationships and need different Routines to induct them into the team's ways of working. They also need to establish a close connection to the team's Reason. When someone leaves a team, they take their knowledge, skills, energy, passion and Relationships with them. This loss creates a shift in the Edge Dynamics in the team which needs to be discussed and addressed. The team needs to determine how to fill the gaps left behind in such a way that new, productive team dynamics are created.

Endings

It's critical for the team to consider how they celebrate endings and capture the knowledge and experience of team members as they leave. This is about ensuring that they leave a legacy behind and do not create a critical failure point in the team by leaving with all that knowledge and experience without the team capturing it first. Leaving is more than just the farewell party. The team should think about all the other things that need to happen when somebody leaves to ensure it is done well.

Beginnings

Inducting new members to the team is also critical. How does the team bring them in and share with them what the team does while at the same time embracing their fresh perspective on the team? How can they build Routines to learn from the experience and ideas of people who are joining the team before they get assimilated into the team? The team has a short window of opportunity for this – probably no more than three months. High-performing teams look forward to new members joining because they relish the challenge of adapting and becoming a refreshed high-performing team.

The experience of good endings and positive beginnings is crucial for the system that your team is part of. When endings are done poorly, the echoes of that person remain in the system and can last for years. Some teams can also carry the pain of the disappearing individual for a long time, especially when someone just vanishes from the team and there was no opportunity to say goodbye properly. In this situation, rumours and speculation will occur as to what happened to that person. Dealing with the ending well ensures that the experience of the team can be managed so that is a good one. It's also about making sure that the team are not creating a critical point of failure. A good ending will ensure that the leaver's information, knowledge and skills is handed over well. Often when somebody leaves a team, we are in a hurry to move on and think about the future without them. We have seen many examples of people leaving teams and in their last few days and weeks they are completely excluded from the team. The team should hold the leaver accountable for creating a positive legacy and impact on the team while at the same time being accountable as a team for enabling a good ending for that person. It is worth the team taking the time to ensure that their ending happens well and the beginning of the new team is a positive one. Teams may feel frustrated that they have invested time and effort developing the person leaving but it is worth coaching the team to notice what opportunities come from their departure. A leaving is always an opportunity to refresh the team.

The lowest scoring Edge Dynamic

When we run a first diagnostic for a team, 99% of the time Resilience is the lowest scoring Edge Dynamic. When we consider why that might be, there are several causes. First of all, Resilience is often an afterthought at the team level – if it's considered at all. Teams are unlikely to look at Resilience beyond thinking about it at the individual level. There may be many resources available within the organization which support individuals in the team to manage and develop their own personal Resilience. In our experience, it's very unusual for teams to think about Resilience together and how to utilize the power of the team. When we first start working with teams, usually team members think about themselves first and the team second. This erodes Resilience and means that team members often don't even notice when their colleagues are struggling. They certainly are not anticipating change, and are not able to identify critical pain points and how the team might need to adapt in the future. Team members who are in this frame of mind often are stuck in the weeds of their own work and don't even notice what's going on around them. When we start to shift their focus from 'me' to 'we', the impacts on Resilience are immediate.

For all of this to happen, vulnerability-based trust is essential. We know that teams need to build reliability-based trust first and vulnerability-based trust comes later once that foundation is in place (see Chapter 11). For there to be strong levels of Resilience in a team, team members need to be able to ask for help, admit they've made mistakes and offer support to others in the team when they need it. They also need to feel comfortable challenging each other and accepting challenge in return. It can be tempting in a team when they get that first diagnostic back to want to start with Resilience – especially when it is the lowest scoring Edge Dynamic. In our experience, this is a mistake and investing in Resilience when the other Edge Dynamics are low is like pushing water uphill. The team should start with the other Edge Dynamics first and resist the temptation to invest lots of time and effort in developing Resilience yet. Doing things in this order will mean that Resilience will improve naturally and the foundation skills will be in place for Resilience to happen. When they then focus on Resilience more deliberately, with strong Edge Dynamics already in place, high performance will be sustainable.

The links to other Edge Dynamics

Resilience is impacted by all the other Edge Dynamics and, as we have noted, is often the lowest scoring Edge Dynamic within a team when we first start coaching them. All the other Edge Dynamics need to be strong for there to be high levels of Resilience in a team. There are also specific impacts on the other Edge Dynamics that are worth paying attention to.

The connection to Reason

When Resilience is high in a team, the team will find it easy to tap into their own personal *why* as well as the team's Reason. They will be more easily motivated and energized and will have the space to maintain line of sight between the work they are doing and the team's purpose. The team uses their Reason to maintain Resilience in tough times.

The connection to Results

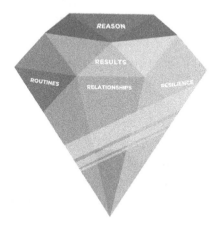

High levels of Resilience undoubtedly lead to excellent Results at both the individual and team level. When the team is seamlessly managing their energy levels and anticipated challenges, Results come easily. They work smarter, not harder.

The connection to Routines

Teams who have strong levels of Resilience have great Routines. The two go hand in hand and influence each other. High-performing teams are constantly learning, adjusting and adapting to change, and this leads to adjusting and adapting Routines regularly to ensure that they are still fit for purpose.

The connection to Relationships

When team Resilience is high, team members feel lower levels of stress – in fact they would describe stress as motivating them to overcome challenges. It has become a positive force for the team. This means that they have the mental and emotional capacity to build and maintain Relationships with their colleagues. Relationships are strengthened by overcoming challenges together.

The case study team

We introduced the case study team to you in Chapter 5, and discussed their context, their aspirations and Advantycs® diagnostic results. Here we will look at the team again in the context of Resilience. The team scored lowest on this Edge Dynamic with 2.7 out of 5. As we've discussed in this chapter, we would not recommend that a team starts their team coaching process by deep diving into Resilience and so we took this approach with the team. The team decided they would like to develop the other four Edge Dynamics first to hopefully impact their team Resilience. And of course this is what happened. Within three months, Resilience increased to 2.9 without any specific effort on this Edge Dynamic. During the team coaching process, a team member left and a new person joined the team. The team came up with a plan to bid fare-well to the exiting team member and to onboard the new one. As part of their induction, they intro-duced them to the team coaching process and the behaviours they had agreed. They shared their values with each other. This integrated the new person into the team coaching process really well and meant they maintained the progress they had made.

Sustaining team Resilience – a summary

Resilience is the team's ability to support each other to bounce forward from adversity even stronger than before. Resilience interacts with Relationships and Routines to support *how* the team operates. Team Resilience is the key to both individual and organizational Resilience and is fundamental for sustaining high performance over long periods of time.

High-performing, resilient teams:

- Do more with what they have
- Work smarter not harder
- Take proper breaks
- Celebrate the small wins
- Laugh together
- Believe there is only winning and learning

If there are high levels of turnover, lots of absence or sickness, we would argue a team has probably got low levels of Resilience. Only the best teams pay close attention to actively managing Resilience at the team level.

The team could use the idea of substitution to maintain Resilience and allow proper breaks from work without productivity dropping.

Resilience doesn't happen by chance, it has to happen by design. The team should design their Routines with Resilience in mind. Challenge them to find strategies and ways of working that are effective for the personalities and needs of the people within the team.

The team should pay attention to the single points of failure. Which critical tasks and skills can only be done by one person in the team? When they are absent, what happens?

The team can create a culture of learning by developing an agile mindset and creating the conditions for experimentation. Team members should consider how to change their perspective regularly and hold up the mirror by reflecting on the Edge Dynamics in the team.

Beginnings and endings are crucial for Resilience; the team should manage new starters and people leaving the team well.

Conclusion

Teams have always been the backbone of organizations, but their landscape is rapidly evolving with the ever-increasing complexity and interconnectedness of the world. Collaboration is now the ultimate competitive advantage, surpassing individual capabilities. However, genuine collaboration remains rare, with only a small percentage of employees contributing substantial value. To thrive in this dynamic environment, organizations must unleash the potential of all team members and foster a collaborative culture. High-performing teams can achieve remarkable results, making collective effort the key to success. It is therefore an exciting time for team coaches – being a part of making such a significant difference to individuals, teams and organizations is hugely satisfying and really takes your coaching capabilities to the next level.

In Chapter 1 we covered the significant differences that set team coaching apart from other team modalities. We discussed your role as a team coach and how important it is to minimize your entanglements and remain objective. We discussed how team coaching takes place over time, forming a strong partnership with the team and their leader. It is an approach led by the team itself, focused on creating sustainable high performance by delving into the team dynamics.

In Chapter 2 we discussed what high performance is and how it is a balance between the objectives of the team and the dynamics within the team. Without both of these a team will not sustain high performance. High-performing teams have huge benefits at the organizational, individual and leadership levels. These benefits include lower staff turnover, increased engagement, higher productivity and greater well-being. We explored how teams don't create high performance by accident, that it happens by design and that this is where you can add huge value as a team coach. Team coaching multiplies the impact you are probably already experiencing through your existing facilitation or individual coaching practice. In fact, it can multiply it exponentially – at least by the number of people in the team, but it also extends out to the wider organization and the team's stakeholders.

In Chapter 3, we discussed how there are a number of core competencies required to be a team coach which build upon the competencies of individual coaching. A team coach must be ethical in their interactions with the team and their stakeholders. They need to consider their own mindset as a coach and the stance that they take in relation to the team and their accountability for their results. They need to set up and maintain clear agreements (contracts) with the team and other stakeholders and recontract when required throughout the process.

An environment of trust and safety is essential in team coaching, as is the coach's ability to maintain presence, listen actively, ask great questions to evoke awareness and enable the team's growth towards high performance.

In Chapter 4, we discussed how to develop your coaching practice, looking at certification and training, accreditation and maintaining your continued coach education. We discussed the benefits of being part of a team coaching community and developing your team coaching toolkit. Receiving supervision is also an essential part of your development as a team coach. We recommend that you broaden your understanding of business models, systems and practices and that you take yourself out of your comfort zone by turning up the heat and creating variety in your development.

Use a framework which supports the team in their thinking about the conditions for high performance. In Chapter 5, we looked at Advantycs®, which consists of a fully integrated, research-based, high-performing team model, toolkit and diagnostic to help team coaches enable the growth of the teams they work with. It comprises the Edge Dynamics of Reason, Results, Routines, Relationships and Resilience, which all work together to create the conditions for high performance in any team. The toolkit supports the development of each of these Edge Dynamics. The diagnostic supports the team to create insight about their dynamics and track their progress.

Teams come in all shapes and sizes and yet some core principles apply to all of them, which we discussed in Chapter 6:

1. Develop the dynamics within the team
2. Create an inclusive culture
3. Increase interdependence
4. Build a sense of untapped potential
5. Celebrate similarities and differences
6. Take a systemic view of the team
7. Sustain high performance

Having one eye on all of these elements ensures that you are coaching the team on the things that will really help them to build high performance and then sustain it.

It's important to have a process for team coaching, and we explored in Chapter 7 the EDGE Team Coaching Process which comprises four stages: Explore, Develop, Generate and Exit. Use this process to structure your team coaching approach.

Team coaching requires you to understand who your client is. If the team is not coachable, don't work with them. Look out for key indicators that this might be the case. Constantly think about how you are interacting with the team and how you are coaching them using the principles of high-performance team coaching.

In Chapter 8, we established that Reason is the team's North Star and is often overlooked as its essence can be 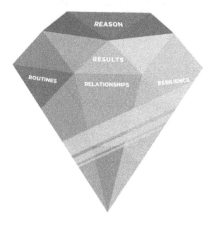 misunderstood. Coach the team to understand that the team Reason is their *why* and is essential for tapping into their motivation to achieve. Without a compelling team Reason, they will not achieve their aspirations, as it's impossible to tap into their full potential without a clear and inspirational *why*.

In Chapter 9, we discussed how it's essential that a team's Results are crystal clear at the individual and team level. This can also easily be overlooked as teams might think that individual objectives are enough. We know that to achieve high performance, teams need a greater clarity of their shared team objectives and the associated measures of success. These need to be Brief, Memorable and Inspirational (BMI) to work. In our experience, you need no more than five 'Big Whats'. Once they have this the team can create the opportunities for collaboration where they add the greatest value.

Routines (Chapter 10) are often where there is an opportunity for quick wins. It doesn't take much for the team to change a meeting cadence or agenda, or to establish a decision-making process. In our experience, Routines become 'fixed' and not fit for purpose just because that's the way things have always been done. Coach the team to continuously ask themselves the question 'why are we doing things this way?' and 'how could we improve this Routine?' Coach them to be prepared to try something out to see if it might work. They should have their own radar for boredom on all the time – notice the signals that their team members may be getting bored with a particular Routine. That's their signal to change it in some way. Coach the team to craft their Routines with the other Edge Dynamics in mind. They should consider how Routines can always be used to build Relationships in the team and should connect to Results and the other Edge Dynamics.

In Chapter 11, we discussed how Relationships are complex in teams because people are complex and so it is important for the team to walk before they can run with their team Relationships. Coach them to make time and opportunities to make enduring connections and a sense of belonging. Coach the team to establish the foundation Relationship skills first before attempting to develop the advanced skills. They will be in danger of damaging their team's Relationships if they try to force the advanced skills too early. Coach them to be patient with this. Little and often is the key to success in their team's Relationships.

We saw in Chapter 12 that Resilience is a fantastic barometer of high performance. It's unusual to have high Resilience and low Reason, Results, Relationships and Routines. Resilience is the key to sustaining high performance and so without it a team's performance will likely be a 'one-off wonder'. Resilience is all about creating a culture of learning. It's about consistently challenging the team to change perspectives and think differently about themselves and their context. Coach the team to be agile and to continuously improve while supporting each other.

What one small step will you take now to develop your team coaching skills and practice? Run a team diagnostic with a team? Use some of the Advantycs® tools? Attend some training on team coaching? Start listening to a podcast about high-performing teams? Take the first step now towards your team coaching edge.

Acknowledgements

Many people have been involved in some way in the writing of this book, so we'll attempt to thank everyone here.

First of all, to our own high-performing team at Management Dynamics, without whose unwavering support, challenge and ideas this book wouldn't have been possible. Peter Firth, India Toller and Emma Lane you challenge us to put into practice what we write and for that we thank you.

To all of our amazing consultants at Management Dynamics who use Advantycs® every day in their work, coaching teams and leaders. Your constructive and often challenging feedback has been and will always be invaluable to us. A particular mention to Nermeen Amr, Anna Slocombe, Monica Hernanz, Tatjana Hartung and Wendy Bedborough who gave detailed feedback and challenged our ideas on the first drafts of the book. A big thank you to Philippe Buyze who not only gave great feedback on the first draft but also provided us with supervision on our team coaching practice. Many valuable insights were generated in those sessions. You all continuously stretch our thinking.

To Carrie Abner from the ICF, thank you for giving us the confidence we were on the right track and confirming this would be a useful guide for team coaches. Thank you, Lawrence Clarke, for your specific feedback on the first draft and the rest of the associate team at Korn Ferry.

We also want to thank the other amazing coaches who have given us feedback and been great support, including Sian Hamson, Michael Levine and Simon Dick.

To all the teams that we've coached over the years, thank you – you've embraced the coaching process, we have loved partnering with you and we've learned so much from you all.

Thank you also to our publisher Alison Jones at Practical Inspiration Publishing, your enthusiasm and energy kept us going and forced us to meet the deadlines.

Finally, we need to acknowledge our wonderful families who we thank for their support and understanding. We dedicate this book to you and hope that Poppy, William, Holly and Ava will be part of wonderful high-performing teams.

Bibliography

Almaatouq, Abdullah, Mohammed Alsobay, Ming Yin and Duncan J. Watts. 'Task complexity moderates group synergy', in *Proceedings of the National Academy of Sciences*, 118 (36), e2101062118 (3 September 2021)

Aube, Caroline, Vincent Rousseau and Sebastien Tremblay. 'Team size and the quality of the group experience. The more the merrier?' in *American Psychological Association*, 15 (4), 357–375 (2011)

Bariso, Justin. 'Google spent years studying effective teams, this single quality contributed most to their success', in *Inc*. Available from: www. inc.com/justin-bariso/google-spent-years-studying-effective-teams-this-single-quality-contributed-most-to-their-success.html Accessed 17 March 2024

Belbin, Meredith. *Management teams: Why they succeed or fail* (2010)

Bender, Lisa et al. 'Social sensitivity correlations with the effectiveness of team process performance, an empirical study', in *ICER '12*, 39–46 (2012)

Blanchard, Ken. *Leading at a higher level: How to be a high-performing leader* (2010)

Buckingham, Marcus and Ashley Goodall. *Nine lies about work* (2019)

Campion, Michael et al. 'Relations between work group characteristics and effectiveness. Implications for designing effective work groups', in *Personnel Psychology*, 46 (4), 823–847 (1993)

Cross, Rob, Reb Rebele and Adam M. Grant. 'Collaborative overload', in *Harvard Business Review* (January 2016). Available from: https://hbsp. harvard.edu/product/R1601E-PDF-ENG Accessed 17 March 2024

Csíkszentmihályi, Mihály. *Flow* (2002)

Dias, Dexter. *The ten types of human* (2018)

Drexler, Allan and David Sibbet. 'Team performance model', *The Grove*. Available from: www.thegrove.com/methodology/team-performance-model Accessed 17 March 2024

Duhigg, Charles. *Smarter, faster, better. The secrets of being productive* (2017)

Duhigg, Charles. *The power of habit* (2013)

Edmondson, Amy. *Teaming. How organizations learn, innovate and compete in the knowledge economy* (2010)

Elliott, Gregory C., Melissa Colangelo and Richard Gelles. 'Mattering and suicide ideation: Establishing and elaborating a relationship', in *Social Psychology Quarterly*, 68 (3), 223–238 (2005)

Emich, K. J. and T. A. Wright. 'The "I"s in team: The importance of individual members to team success', in *Organizational Edge Dynamics*, 45, 2–10 (2016)

Ernst & Young. *The power of many: How companies use teams to drive superior corporate performance* (2013)

Gersick, C. 'Marking time: Predictable transitions in task groups', in *Academy of Management Journal*, 32 (2), 9–41 (1989)

Gilbert, Andrew and Karen Whittleworth. *OSCAR coaching model: Simplifying workplace coaching* (2009).

Grenny, Joseph. 'The best teams hold themselves accountable', in *Harvard Business Review* (May 2014). Available from: https://hbr.org/2014/05/the-best-teams-hold-themselves-accountable Accessed 17 March 2024

Guttman, Howard. *Great business teams: Cracking the code for standout performance* (2008)

Hackman, J. Richard. *Leading teams: Setting the stage for great performances* (2002)

Hall, Kevan and Alan Hall. *Kill bad meetings* (2017)

Hanlan, Marc. *High performance teams: How to make them work* (2004)

Hawkins, Peter. *Creating a coaching culture* (2012).

de Jong, Bart et al. 'Trust and team performance: A meta analysis of main effects, contingencies and qualifiers', in *Academy of Management Annual Proceedings*, 2015 (1), 14561 (2015)

Katzenbach, J. R. *Peak performance* (2000)

Katzenbach, Jon R. and Douglas K. Smith. *The wisdom of teams* (1993)

Kegan, Robert and Lisa Lahey. *Everyone culture* (2016)

Knapp, Kane and John Zeratsky. *Sprint: How to solve big problems and test new ideas in just 5 days* (2016)

Kramer, S. and T. Amabile. 'The power of small wins', in *Harvard Business Review* (May 2011)

Lahey, Lisa and Robert Kegan. *Immunity to change* (2009)

Larson, Erik. 'New research: Diversity + inclusion = better decision making at work', in *Forbes* (2017). Available from: www.forbes.com/sites/eriklarson/2017/09/21/new-research-diversity-inclusion-better-decision-making-at-work/#285cd6e74cbf Accessed 17 March 2024

Lencioni, Patrick. *The 5 dysfunctions of a team* (2002)

Lynn, Gary S. and Faruk Kalay. 'The effect of vision and role clarity on team performance', in *Journal of Business, Economics and Finance*, 4 (3), (2015)

Marlow, Shannon, Christina Lacerenza, Jensine Paoletti, Shawn Burke and Eduardo Salas. 'Does team communication represent a one-size for all approach? A meta-analysis of team communication and performance', in *Organizational Behavior and Human Decision Processes*, 144(4), 145–170 (2018)

Mathieu, John, M. Travis Maynard and Tammy Rapp. 'Team effectiveness 1997–2007: A review of recent advancements and a glimpse into the future', in *Journal of Management*, 34 (3) (2008)

Matthews, Gail. 'Study focuses on strategies for achieving goals', Dominican University of California (2015)

McAdams, Dan and Ed de St Aubin. 'A theory of generativity and its assessment through self-report, behavioral acts, and narrative themes in autobiography', in *Journal of Personality and Social Psychology*, 62 (6), 1003–1015 (1992)

Moreland, Richard and John Levine. 'Group socialization: Theory and research', in *European Review of Social Psychology*, 5 (1), 305–336 (1994)

Moreland, Richard and John Levine. 'Socialization in small groups: Temporal changes in individual-group relations', in *Advances in Experimental Social Psychology*, 15, 137–192 (1982)

Moreland, Richard L., John M. Levine and Melissa L. Wingert. *Creating the ideal group: Composition effects at work* (1996)

Naquin, Charles E. and Reynee O. Tynan. 'Team halo effect: Why teams are not blamed for their failures', in *Journal of Applied Psychology*, 88 (2), 332–340 (2003)

Pentland, Alex 'Sandy'. 'The new science of building great teams', in *Harvard Business Review* (April 2012). Available from: https://hbr.org/2012/04/the-new-science-of-building-great-teams Accessed 17 March 2024

Polzer, Jeffrey T. et al. 'Capitalizing on diversity: Interpersonal congruence in small work groups', in *Administrative Science Quarterly*, 47 (2), 296–324 (2002)

Rosenberg, M. and B. McCullough. 'Mattering: Inferred significant and mental health among adolescents', in *Research in Community and Mental Health*, 2, 163–182 (2005)

Ryan, Richard and Edward L. Deci. 'Self-determination theory and the facilitation of intrinsic motivation, social development, and well-being', in *American Psychologist*, 55 (1), 68–78 (2000)

Sinek, Simon. *Start with why. How great leaders inspire everyone to take action* (2011)

Sundstrom, Eric, Kenneth P. de Meuse and David Futrell. 'Work teams: Applications and effectiveness', in *American Psychologist*, 45 (2), 120–133 (1990)

Susskind, Richard. *The future of the professions: How technology will transform the work of human experts* (2017)

Swann, William B. et al. 'Finding value in diversity: Verification of personal and social self-views in diverse groups', in *Academy of Management Review*, 29 (1), 9–27 (2004)

Tabrizi, Behnam. '75% of cross-functional teams are dysfunctional', in *Harvard Business Review* (June 2015). Available from: https://hbr.org/2015/06/75-of-cross-functional-teams-are-dysfunctional Accessed 17 March 2024

Tuckman, Bruce. *Stages of team development model* (1965)

UK Department of Trade and Industry. *High performance workplaces – informing and consulting employees* (2003)

Whitmore, John. *Coaching for performance, the principles and practice of coaching and leadership* (2017)

Wiseman, Liz. *Multipliers: How the best leaders make everyone smart* (2017)

Witt, David. *60% of work teams fail – top 10 reasons why.* Available from: https://leaderchat.org/2011/11/03/60-of-work-teams-fail-top-10-reasons-why/ Accessed 17 March 2024

Woolley, Anita Williams et al. 'Evidence for a collective intelligence factor in the performance of human groups', *Science*, 330 (6004), 686–688 (2010)

Index